IMAGES
of America

ASIAN INDIANS
OF CHICAGO

Following a 1949 address to faculty and students at the University of Chicago, Jawaharlal Nehru, India's first Prime Minister (1947–1964) left Rockefeller Chapel escorted by University Marshal Harold Anderson. Nehru was accompanied by his daughter, Indira Gandhi, who also served as Prime Minister (1966–1977, 1980–1984). During his two-day visit, University officials arranged for a sampling of life in the Midwest with tours of three working farms in Yorkville, Illinois. Years before they were a significant presence in the U.S., Nehru's visit foreshadowed a future in which Asian Indians would thrive in Chicago. (Courtesy of University of Chicago Library Special Collections Research Center.)

Cover: Chicago's Asian Indian community joined the celebrations when the city hosted the 1994 World Cup soccer championship. The festivities included the Parade of Nations on Michigan Avenue with dancers Krithika Rajagopalan (left) and Sreepadma Priya Sonty on the Indian float. (Courtesy of India Tribune.)

IMAGES
of America

ASIAN INDIANS OF CHICAGO

Indo-American Center

ARCADIA
PUBLISHING

Published by Arcadia Publishing
Charleston, South Carolina

Library of Congress Catalog Card Number: 2002106138

For all general information contact Arcadia Publishing at:
Telephone 843-853-2070
Fax 843-853-0044
E-Mail sales@arcadiapublishing.com
For customer service and orders:
Toll-Free 1-888-313-2665

Visit us on the Internet at www.arcadiapublishing.com

Dressed in his World War I uniform and carrying his officer's ceremonial sword, Chandra Lachman Singh and his wife Nerissa pose in front of the Armory building at 57th and Cottage Grove in 1926. Singh came to the U.S. in 1911 from Grenada and worked in Chicago before being inducted into the army in 1918. After the war, he returned to Chicago where he purchased and managed residential properties, first in Lincoln Park and later in Hyde Park until his death in 1989. From 1929 to 1932, the Singhs worked in India with Gandhi and the Indian National Congress in the independence movement. In 1950, Nerissa Singh became the first woman of Indian origin to earn a medical degree from Chicago Medical School. (Courtesy of Sheila and Aspy Tantra.)

CONTENTS

Acknowledgments   6

About the Authors   7

Introduction   9

1.   The Early Years: A Spirit of Adventure   11

2.   Occupations: Earning a Living   21

3.   Family Life: Preservation and Adaptation   33

4.   Religion: Keeping the Faith   43

5.   Devon Avenue: Ethnic Marketplace   57

6.   Arts: Tradition and Transformation   69

7.   Entertainment: Sport and Pastime   81

8.   Politics: Getting Involved   91

9.   Service: Fulfilling Needs   101

10.   Homeland: Strengthening Links   111

Select Readings and Films about Asian Indian Immigrants   125

About the Indo-American Center   127

ACKNOWLEDGMENTS

This pictorial history of Chicago's Asian Indian community comprises the contributions of hundreds of people. To all those involved in creating this unique book, we offer our deepest appreciation. Along with scores who responded to our appeal for pictures, there were many others working behind the scenes identifying people in the photographs, tracking down accurate historical information, and urging friends to scour their personal archives for relevant documents. Although we have attempted to be as representative and inclusive as possible, space constraints prevented us from using all of the photos offered by several generous individuals.

The support of certain individuals and organizations has been particularly significant and we would like to express our gratitude to them. Mukul Roy, unofficial photographer laureate of the Asian Indian community since the 1970s, gave generously of her photographs, which have outstanding historic and aesthetic value. She graciously tolerated the unavoidable cropping of many of her pictures and spent many hours helping us select the most appropriate photographs from the community. Another veteran of the Chicago scene, Urmilla Chawla, onetime photojournalist, Indian TV personality, and active member of many charitable organizations, gave us free run of her photographs, collected over three decades. We owe special thanks to B.S. Subbakrishna whose photographs of the built environment helped to fill many gaps in the book. Other individuals and organizations who contributed photos are acknowledged in the captions. Those who also assisted us with detailed information include Prem Sharma, Gyan Agarwal, Hector Lobo, Gouri Sen, Kiran Chaturvedi, Nafisa and Mannan Bandukwala, C.K. Chandran, Rajendran Raja, Naseem Umar, Mohammad Mandur, Jim Kenney, Travis Rejman, M.S. Saini, Roshan Rivetna, Ratan Sharma, P. Rajagopalan, Ashok Easwaran, and Sheila and Aspy Tantra. We also thank the Indo-American Center Board and staff members including Executive Director R.S. Rajan, Intern Bindhu Vijayan, Faisal Hadi, and Gita Chawla.

As a repository of the community's history, the ethnic media has been an invaluable resource. *India Tribune*, the Chicago Asian Indian community's oldest continuing English newspaper has covered local events for the past 26 years, and its publisher and editor, Prashant Shah, along with J.V. Lakshmana Rao, was most gracious in allowing us to use the newspaper archives. We thank Samantha Gleisten of Arcadia Publishing for her skilful editing and sensitive stewardship of this project.

When we embarked on this endeavor, we little knew that it would involve such extensive outreach and perseverance. Our husbands, who bore the brunt of our preoccupation with this project, have shown great forbearance and we truly appreciate their support. Most of all, we thank the community for enabling us to produce this historical work. It has been an immeasurably rewarding task for us. We hope that you, the reader, will find this introduction to Chicago's thriving Asian Indian community enlightening and enjoyable, and that our efforts will spur others to delve further into our community's history.

The Indo-American Center Education Committee

ABOUT THE AUTHORS

The authors of this book, listed below in alphabetical order, are members of the Indo-American Center Board of Directors and serve on its Education Committee. The Education Committee organizes programs to increase understanding and appreciation of Indian heritage and culture. Through the Center's Ethnic Outreach sessions it offers visiting groups and classes an introduction to the culture and history of India and the immigrant community. Its teachers' workshops help educators to include an Indian component in their existing curriculum at all grade levels. It works with institutions in the city to further awareness of Chicago's Indian American community and its heritage.

LAKSHMI MENON is past president of the Indo-American Center and an active spokesperson for Chicago's Indian-American community. Her writing and media skills have brought her wide recognition both in the Indian community and the broader mainstream society. Her ability to interpret Indian culture for a wide audience has made her a well-known representative of the Indian community, a role she fulfills through many hours of volunteer service. She is often featured in or consulted by the *Chicago Tribune* and *Sun Times*, national public radio and television, and many of the city's institutions for programs about Indians in Chicago.

PADMA RANGASWAMY is an historian, author, past president of the Indo-American Center, and active member of Chicago's Asian Indian community. Her book, *Namasté America: Indian Immigrants in an American Metropolis* (Pennsylvania State University Press, 2000) is a comprehensive study of Asian Indian immigration. She has also contributed several entries to Asian-American encyclopedias. She has taught World History, American History, and Asian American History at many universities including the University of Illinois at Chicago, Loyola University, North Central College, Dominican University, and Northwestern University. She served as coordinator of the *My History Is Your History* Project at the Chicago Historical Society. Her current research for DePaul University's The New Chicago project focuses on the Devon Avenue marketplace and the Indian-American community in Chicago.

DOROTHIE SHAH is Education Project Coordinator and Executive Board Member at the Indo-American Center in Chicago. For two decades she taught high school history and social science at Evanston Township High School where she developed courses which introduced hundreds of students to India, China, and Japan. She has served as an Educational Consultant to the South Asia Outreach Educational Project at the University of Chicago, Evenings for Educators Program at the Art Institute of Chicago, and the Chicago Historical Society. Her interest in the Asian immigrant community grew out of experiences with her husband, who is an Asian Indian immigrant from Mumbai (Bombay) and his family. Shah and Rangaswamy are co-authors of a unit on *Asian Immigration to the United States* for the Organization of American Historians.

The authors of this book are solely responsible for its contents.

ASIAN INDIAN POPULATION
CHICAGO METRO AREA
1980–2000

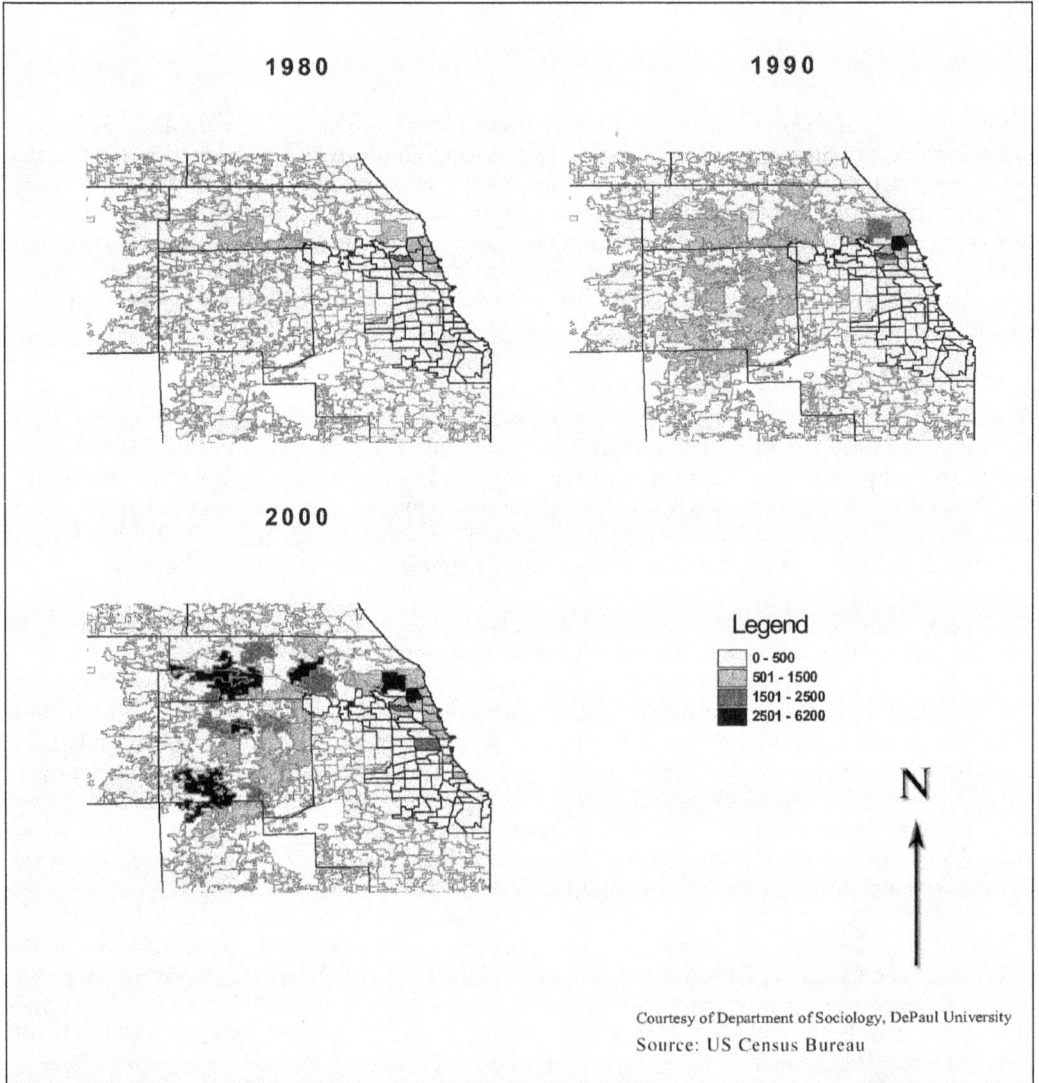

Courtesy of Department of Sociology, DePaul University

Source: US Census Bureau

In 1980, when Asian Indians were first counted as a distinct group in the U.S. Census, they numbered 31,858 in the six-county Chicago metropolitan area, comprising Cook, DuPage, Kane, Lake, McHenry, and Will counties. The population distribution showed a small concentration in the northside neighborhoods of Chicago and a scattered presence in the near northwest suburbs. The 1990 census showed further expansion in these areas, with the Asian Indian population increasing to 57,992. By 2000, Asian Indians numbered 113,700 in these six counties, registering significant growth throughout the metropolitan area.

INTRODUCTION

The story of immigrants from India who settled in the Chicago area is a relatively recent chapter in the history of the United States. Indian immigration was not a flight from war, famine, or oppression, but a movement driven by opportunity in America, fueled by circumstances in newly independent India, and shaped by enduring ties to the motherland.

The first significant number of immigrants from India (also known as Asian Indians or Indian Americans) arrived in the United States between 1900 and 1910, when about 7,000 members of the Sikh community from the Punjab came to California. A series of anti-Asian legislative measures led to a steady decline in immigration from India until, with the Barred Zone Act of 1917, it was cut off completely. The Luce-Cellar Bill of 1946 granted Indians citizenship rights and allotted India a quota of 100 immigrants per annum. As a result of this quota, by 1960, according to Indians present at the time, there were about 350 of them living in Chicago. Most of them had come as students, but a few obtained jobs and settled here, becoming the nucleus of a community which numbered 113,700 in the six-county Chicago metro area according to the 2000 census.

This huge increase began with the easing of restrictions when the United States Congress passed the 1965 Immigration and Nationality Act, which abolished the national origins quota and granted visas to persons with special skills needed in the U.S. Because of the Cold War with the USSR and the war in Vietnam, physicians, engineers, and scientists were in short supply. Substantial numbers of professionally qualified Indians came to Chicago and other U.S. cities to remedy this shortage. They helped staff the nation's hospitals, design its infrastructure, drive its research programs, and teach its students, gaining valuable experience and professional expertise in the process.

The majority of Indians who came to the U.S. in the 1960s and 1970s considered themselves sojourners rather than immigrants intending to remain permanently. Most belonged to the first post-independence generation and had not yet invested themselves heavily in careers in India. Although they represented the tremendous linguistic, religious, and cultural diversity of their native land, they were fluent in English and familiar with Western systems of thought thanks to the British colonial legacy. Thanks also to exposure to Hollywood movies, they were filled with curiosity about life in America, and responded with enthusiasm to U.S. recruitment efforts. They fully intended to return to the responsibilities of their lives in India after two or three years abroad. Their prevailing mood upon arrival was one of discovery and exhilaration.

These early immigrants were highly regarded in their professions and were offered ample attractive opportunities for advancing their careers. By the time their self-imposed deadlines for returning to India drew to a close, the U.S. free enterprise system had worked its magic on this group. They found little appeal in India's socialist form of government and its bureaucracy.

Thus these sojourners began to settle down and build a community in Chicago. They scattered across the metropolitan area, choosing to live in neighborhoods close to work with good schools for their children. In an effort to teach the next generation about its heritage, they began to form cultural and religious organizations during the 1970s. A fledgling newspaper in English (the only language common to all the Indians here) and a radio and television program were the harbingers of the media onslaught that would spring up to keep them abreast of news, fashion trends, and entertainment from India. In the early 1970s, a sari shop, a grocery store, and a few Indian restaurants began offering Asian Indians some of the comforts of home.

By the mid 1980s, relatives sponsored under the family reunification clause of the Immigration Act of 1965 began to arrive in Chicago. Although students and professionals continued to come in steady numbers, many of these other newcomers were unskilled, spoke little English, and lacked exposure to the western world. They derived comfort from each other as they negotiated their strange new world, and many settled into the Rogers Park neighborhood near Devon Avenue, where ethnic shops were readily accessible. By 1990, one in twelve residents of the area was of Indian origin. Many of these non-professional immigrants relied on their already established relatives who set them up with franchises or small businesses, which served the prosperous Asian Indian population.

This led to a period of vigorous commercial growth along Devon Avenue where shuttered stores and neglected spaces offered new entrepreneurs a perfect venue. Soon the street was transformed into a vibrant array of sari shops, jewelry, music and video stores, groceries, and restaurants. From modest beginnings in 1973 the Indian business district on Devon Avenue became one of the largest ethnic commercial districts in the U.S.

With the unprecedented growth in the Indian immigrant community during the 1980s, especially along the research and high-tech corridors in Chicago's northern and western suburbs, temples, mosques, and businesses catering to Indians sprang up in those areas. Immigration continued at a rapid pace during the 1990s as companies recruited computer professionals from India. By the time the millennium rolled to a close, more than 72 percent of the immigrants from India lived in suburbs of Chicago rather than within the city limits.

If the 1960s and 70s could be characterized as a period of discovery and the 80s as the period of explosive growth, the 90s may well be viewed as the time of consolidation and assessment in the Indian immigrant community. Institutions and organizations that were founded during the preceding decade became firmly established in the social and cultural landscape of Chicago. Until this time, the community had created associations catering to its diverse religious and leisure-time interests. However, in the 1990s, immigrants became aware of needs within their community and established organizations to deal with a variety of issues. Non-profit agencies helped immigrants who were less skilled and in need of support as they adjusted to their new homeland. Individuals and organizations began to take a more active role in the political life of the city. Professional associations were established to assist fellow countrymen in a variety of fields, and the second generation, while wholeheartedly identifying themselves as American, became comfortable about embracing their heritage and formed organizations of their own.

The 2000 census showed that Indian Americans numbered 124,723 in Illinois and constituted the largest Asian American group in the Chicago metro area. Although differences in language, religious and cultural traditions, and educational and income levels challenge the very concept of community, the Indian American population has nevertheless acquired a distinctive identity, building institutions and creating networks to sustain itself as a new American-born generation reaches adulthood. Modern technological developments and the ease of travel and communication in the 20th century have helped the immigrants maintain strong links to their land of origin, drawing sustenance from their heritage as they join the American mainstream.

One

THE EARLY YEARS
A SPIRIT OF ADVENTURE

Long before the vigorous growth of an Asian Indian immigrant population in the mid-1960s, some famous Indians such as the great Hindu philosopher Swami Vivekananda and Bengali Nobel Laureate Rabindranath Tagore visited and left their mark on Chicago. After World War II, students and academics arrived in small numbers. Most were on Indian government scholarships and were required to return upon completion of their studies. Students arriving in the 1950s enjoyed the hospitality of Chandra and Nerissa Singh who were among the earliest settlers of Indian origin in Chicago. In the early 1960s, short-term visitors to the U.S. included some 45 Indian engineers who were brought to Inland Steel and U.S. Steel for training in running newly constructed steel mills in India. After 1965, Indians arrived in large numbers and formed the first substantial Asian Indian population in Chicago. The selective nature of the 1965 immigration law gave initial preference to skilled professionals but once established, these professionals sponsored their relatives and the community became much more diverse.

Indian students, pictured here on Midway Plaisance in front of International House at the University of Chicago in June 1946, were among the first Indians to arrive in Chicago. Since their visas did not permit them to reenter the U.S. once they left, some chose to forgo the opportunity to return home, and eventually became the very first Indian immigrants of the modern era. (Courtesy of C.K. Chandran.)

On September 15, 1893, Swami Vivekananda (front, third from left), appeared on a platform at the Art Institute of Chicago with (seated, left to right) Virchand Gandhi, a Jain scholar, H. Dharmapala, a Buddhist monk from Ceylon (Sri Lanka), and other dignitaries at the World's Parliament of Religions. In his famous electrifying speech, the striking "Hindoo monk of India" proclaimed that truth is one and that all religions are valid means of realizing the one truth. *The New York Herald* wrote of him, "After hearing Swami Vivekananda, we feel how foolish it is to send missionaries to this learned nation." The Swami stayed with Mr. and Mrs. George W. Hale of 1415 N. Dearborn Street. As a result of his frequent Midwest visits, the Vedanta Society of Chicago was established in Hyde Park in 1930. It remains one of the oldest religious institutions in the U.S. devoted to the teaching of ancient Hindu philosophy. (Courtesy of the Vedanta Society of St. Louis.)

When Chicago celebrated the 100th anniversary of the World's Parliament of Religions in 1993, the Vedanta Society bought a statue of Swami Vivekananda for installation in Grant Park but for political reasons the city declined to honor its commitment. In 1998, the statue was given to the Hindu Temple of Greater Chicago, where at the dawn of the 21st century, it stands as a remarkable symbol of continuity and inspiration for Chicago's Hindus. (Photo by B.S. Subbakrishna.)

Rabindranath Tagore (1861–1941) (seated center), who was the first Asian to receive a Nobel Prize (for Literature in 1913), visited the University of Illinois at Urbana, where his son was studying agriculture. Here he met the Tagore Circle members at 909 W. Nevada, Urbana, in the home of Mr. and Mrs. Arthur. R. Seymour (standing, fourth from right and seated, fourth from left) in December 1916. He read from his works to Circle members and lectured at the University of Chicago. His best known work, *Gitanjali*, brought him fame in America, and six poems from that collection were published in the Chicago magazine "Poetry," the first journal in America to publish his poems. (Courtesy of the Champaign-Urbana News Gazette and the University Archives, University of Illinois at Urbana-Champaign.)

Subrahmanyam Chandrasekhar (1910–1995) described as the "greatest mathematical astrophysicist of our generation" had a long and distinguished career at the University of Chicago where he first accepted a faculty position in 1937. He opted to remain in Chicago after agonizing over an invitation from India's Prime Minister Jawaharlal Nehru to return to his newly independent homeland to head the nation's science program. He was awarded the Nobel Prize for Physics in 1983 for his work on the nature of stars and black holes. He was widely admired not only for his award-winning scientific research but also for his deep and wide knowledge of literature and the arts. The world's most powerful X-ray telescope launched by NASA is named the Chandra X-Ray Observatory in his honor. (Courtesy of Lalitha Chandrasekhar.)

Picnics at the Indiana Dunes State Park were a popular pastime for the early Indian students. Women wore their traditional saris at this June 14, 1959 picnic, just as they would in India for informal outdoor events. (Courtesy of Gouri Sen.)

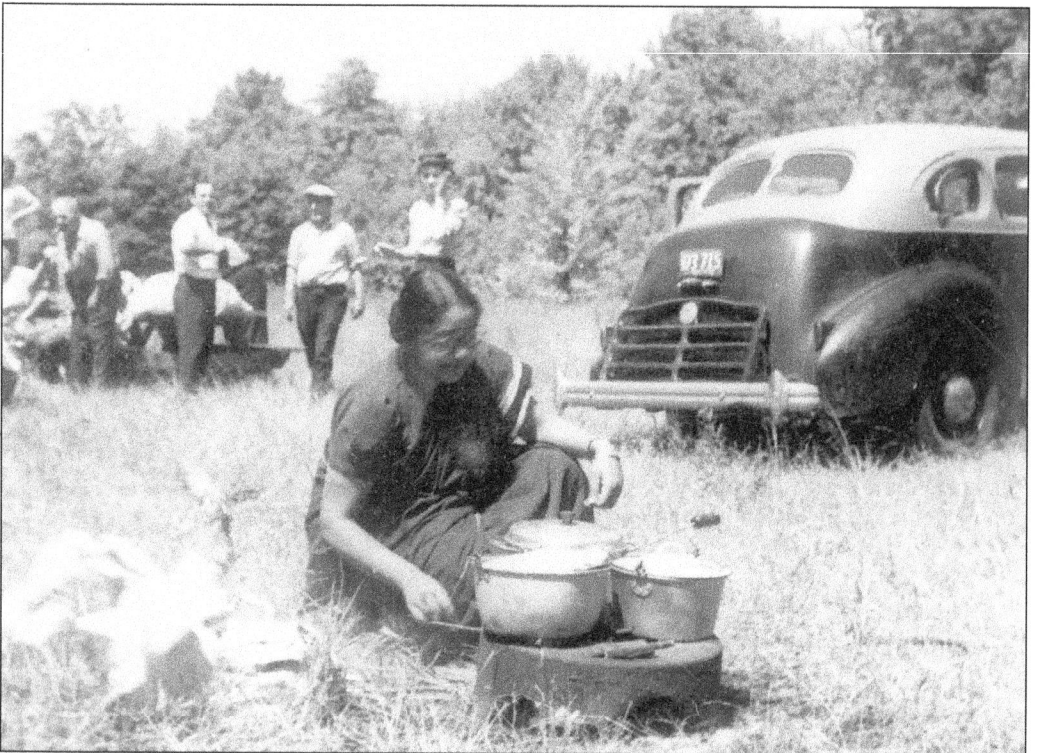

A central feature of the student picnics was the cooking of Indian food. Dr. Banerji of the Sociology Department of the University of Chicago tends to dishes for a 1946 gathering that brought back the taste of home. (Courtesy of C.K. Chandran.)

Student tourists (from front left, clockwise) C.K. Chandran, A. Srinivasan, Suresh Patel, Majhi, and B. Ramakrishna relax by a rock downstream of Niagara. According to Chandran, he and Patel "bought and operated a large car, Oldsmobile-6" (which occasionally broke down!) "in 1946-47, and traveled around the Midwest, taking other Indian students along as paying guests." Chandran went on to a career in the Indian government and now spends his retirement with his American-educated children in Maryland. (Courtesy of C.K. Chandran.)

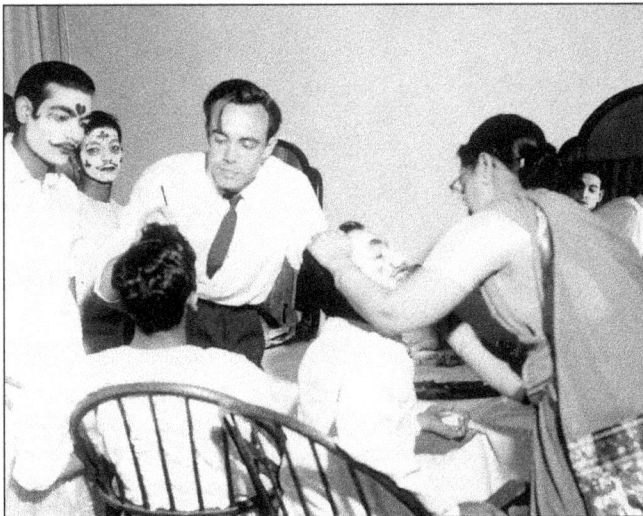

Students apply makeup for a Bengali play staged in May 1961. Activities of Indian students ranged from cultural celebrations, featuring dance, music, and drama to educational programs, discussions, and debates on world issues. Because most Indians were on temporary student visas, they saw themselves as ambassadors representing their own culture at international student gatherings rather than as immigrants assimilating to American ways. (Courtesy of Gouri Sen.)

M.C. Chagla, India's Ambassador to the United States (1958–1961) (right) delivered the inaugural address at a convention of Indian Students of the Midwest at University of Chicago International House in 1960. He is accompanied by Mannan Bandukwala, Convention Chair (left) and L.R. Sethi, Educational and Cultural Counselor to the Ambassador (center). Students from universities throughout the midwest, as well as Illinois Institute of Technology and Northwestern University, participated. (Courtesy of Mannan Bandukwala.)

Blue of Bengal

Serene new shade of HS&M suits of the world's best—pure virgin wool. East meets West to create fashion news in HS&M's Chanda Bengaline suit. The new blue in an all-wool-worsted of Indian ancestry. Advanced styling—double-piped pockets, side vents.

Years before Gap stores began featuring multi-ethnic models in their advertisements, Nafisa (far left) and Mannan Bandukwala (far right) of Palos Park appeared in a 1967 Time magazine ad with professional models (center) for the Hart Schaffner & Marx line of Bengal Blue suits. (Courtesy of Mannan Bandukwala.)

Like thousands of others who came to the U.S. to study, Surendra P. Shah found the allure of research in America captivating. After he completed his doctorate at Cornell University, he began an academic career at the University of Illinois in Chicago where he is shown conducting tests in the materials engineering laboratory in 1968. In 1981, he joined the Civil Engineering faculty at Northwestern University, where he became director of the National Science Foundation Science and Technology Center on Advanced Cement-Based Materials. (Courtesy of Dorothie Shah.)

Many of the professional Indians who came in the first wave did so in a spirit of adventure and excitement, confident that they would soon return to their homeland. Here, the mother of a Chicago area cardiologist, Arvind Menon, congratulates her son on having passed his cardiology board exam and assumes he will come home after his training. In a letter dated May 29, 1974, she writes, "So my little Unni is now a great cardiologist! How happy and proud I am! … I suppose this qualification is enough to hold the highest position in this subspecialty in any teaching institution. When you come home after a few months you must make a good probe and see if you can get into any … such institutions in our own country." Twenty eight years after this letter was written, Dr. Menon remains a Chicago area resident, though, like other Indians, he does visit India frequently. (Courtesy of Lakshmi Menon.)

17

Sadhna Agarwal cooks an Indian meal in the family home in Oak Park in the 1970s while her daughter looks on. Indian women who accompanied their husbands maintained their traditional dress and cuisine when they first arrived. Many of them were professionals who worked outside the home. Sadhna, who was educated as a lawyer in India, subsequently pursued a business career in the United States. (Courtesy of Gyan Agarwal.)

These advertisements for products much sought after by the early Indians appeared in the March 1970 publication of *India Forum*, an organization devoted to the exchange of ideas and information about India. In the early days, Indian restaurants and stores were a rarity. The availability of Indian restaurant food was welcomed by both Asian Indians and adventurous Americans. Before any shop offered saris, an immigrant established an import outlet in his home. Those who desired Indian spices or other ingredients such as lentils much used in Indian cooking had to send for them via mail from New York or shop in specialty stores like Conte De Savoia. (Courtesy of Gyan Agarwal.)

Lisa and Ann Lata Kalayil take part in a 12-hour festival held in 1969 at Grant Park to mark the 100th anniversary of the October 2nd birthday of India's freedom fighter and Father of the Nation, Mahatma Gandhi. A poster of Gandhi, garlanded Indian-style as a mark of honor, adorns the stage. Indians have always maintained strong links to the homeland and to this day, *Gandhi Jayanti* is marked in Chicago by the Indian community with events celebrating his commitment to peace, non-violence, and freedom. This was one of the earliest Indian events to be held in a public venue in Chicago. (Courtesy of Ann Lata Kalayil.)

Affirming patriotic connections with their new homeland, Chicago area Indians participate in the 1976 Bicentennial parade on State Street. (Courtesy of Ann Lata Kalayil.)

In 1972, a small group of Asian Indians established the India League of America (ILA) to promote mutual understanding between Indian immigrants and the American community. Its history is archived at the Chicago Historical Society. ILA Board members gather in 1995 at the opening of an exhibition of Indian paintings at University of Chicago Smart Museum of Art. Pictured (from left) are Shobhana Sanghvi, Indra Goel, Krishna Puranmulka, Roshan Goel, Kimerly Rorschach (Director, Smart Museum), Madan Singh, Sonia Singh, Sunita Puranmulka, Shelly Sinha, K.R. Sinha (Consul General of India), Ralph Nicholas, Barbara Rossi (Curator of Exhibition), Niru Parikh, Ellen Parikh, Manoj Sanghvi, Hekmat Jha, Marta Nicholas, and Chandra Jha. (Courtesy of ILA.)

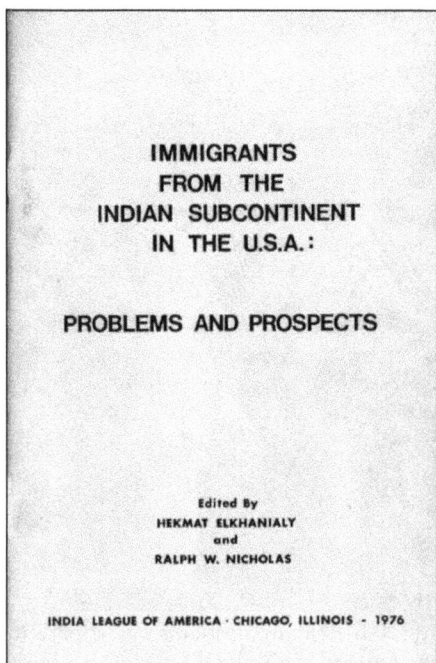

IMMIGRANTS
FROM THE
INDIAN SUBCONTINENT
IN THE U.S.A.:

PROBLEMS AND PROSPECTS

Edited By
HEKMAT ELKHANIALY
and
RALPH W. NICHOLAS

INDIA LEAGUE OF AMERICA · CHICAGO, ILLINOIS · 1976

Before Asian Indians were counted as a separate minority for the very first time in the 1980 U.S. Census, there was considerable controversy in the community as to whether they should be called a "minority" at all. This report was the result of an ILA-sponsored 1976 study of Chicago area immigrants which showed that 70 percent of the 150 respondents preferred to call themselves "brown," not "black" or "white," and approximately three-quarters preferred minority status. Indian organizations such as Association of Indians in America lobbied vigorously for minority status. Gaining separate minority status enabled Indians to track their own growth as an immigrant population in quantitative terms as well as to organize themselves and form effective coalitions with other groups.

Two

OCCUPATIONS
EARNING A LIVING

The Indian community that began to establish itself in and around Chicago during the 1960s consisted almost entirely of scientists, engineers, physicians, academicians, and other professionals and their families. The community began to reflect more economic diversity during the period of explosive growth in the 1980s as the early arrivals sent for other family members and helped less-skilled relatives open small businesses that provided ethnic services and goods. Of these later arrivals, many entered the sales force of mainstream insurance companies, real estate agencies, and brokerage houses that saw the potential in marketing to the Asian Indian ethnic group. Others who spoke little English joined the blue collar workforce as taxi drivers, factory workers and shop assistants.

During the 1980s and 90s, many Indian immigrants ventured beyond the institutions of their employers, utilizing their unique combination of entrepreneurial energy, professional training, and global connections to establish international commercial and technical enterprises of their own. The onset of the information age in the 1990s brought yet another surge in the community's growth with the arrival of large numbers of computer-related professionals from India. As the decade progressed, a plethora of Indians rose to the top levels of management in the corporate and consulting world. Many members of the younger generation began to resist the stereotypical science track and entered the fields of law and the arts.

The Chicago engineering firm of Sargent and Lundy employed large numbers of Indians who had graduated from area universities as well as engineers who had arrived from India during the 1960s and 1970s. Many of these engineers have assumed leadership positions in the immigrant community. (Photo by Mukul Roy.)

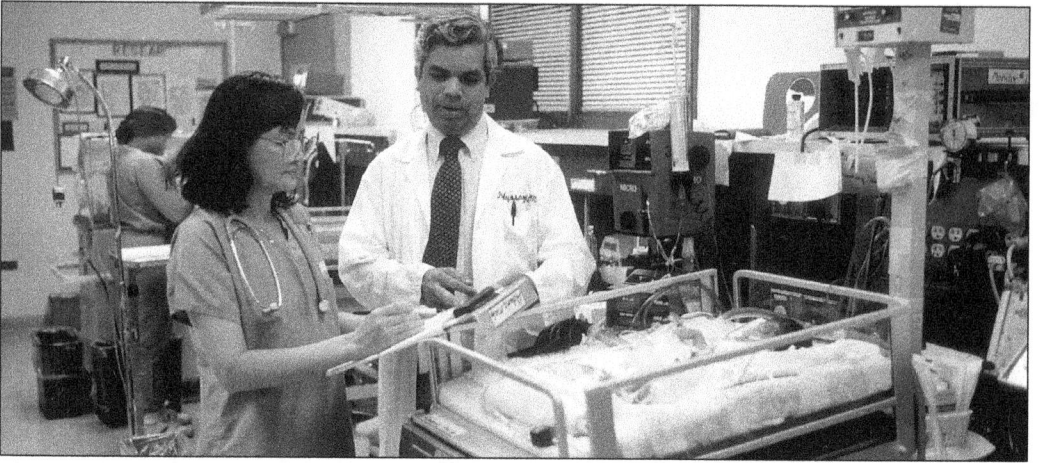

Physicians constituted a major segment of the first Indian immigration wave. Dr. Dharmapuri Vidyasagar, Director of Neonatology at the University of Illinois at Chicago, helped establish the department at the UIC Hospital. His pioneering efforts in establishing training programs to improve neonatal care in developing nations have won international recognition. As the first president of the Hindu Temple of Greater Chicago, he was also instrumental in shaping the course of a major spiritual institution. (Photo by Mukul Roy.)

Dr. Rajendran Raja (inset) and coworkers assemble for an event marking the 1992 start of the DO experiment data gathering at Fermilab in Batavia. The Indian flag (fourth from left) is displayed among the flags of nations whose scientists collaborated on the project. Dr. Raja, the first Indian physicist at Fermilab, joined the institution in 1975 and attracted active participation from premier research institutions in India. Indian scientists played a significant role in the 1995 breakthrough discovery of the top quark, a fundamental constituent of matter that was abundant at the beginning of the universe. (Courtesy of Fermilab.)

Avan Billimoria (center) shares a light moment with Illinois poet laureate Gwendolyn Brooks (left) and Nobel Laureate author Toni Morrison during her 1997-1998 term as Chicago State University Acting President. Indian women came as graduate students or accompanied their husbands to Chicago, joined academic programs upon arrival, and went on to distinguished careers in a variety of fields including medicine, business, science, and social work. (Courtesy of Avan Billimoria.)

The Chicago area offered Indian professionals opportunities in a wide range of fields. Following her tenure as Chicago Public Library administrator, Ranjana Bhargava (left) became Executive Director of Apna Ghar, a South Asian domestic violence shelter. In 1990, she was joined by colleague Robert Remer; historian Ronald Takaki, author of a book on Asian immigrants, *Strangers from a Different Shore*; and library administrator Charlotte Kim following a lecture by Takaki at the Chicago Cultural Center. (Courtesy of *India Tribune*.)

One of the early Indian entrepreneurs, Alfa Manufacturing Industries, Inc. President Diljit S. Ahluwalia (second from left), established his business in Skokie in 1977. In 1990, Illinois Treasurer Patrick Quinn (center) announced a financing package to fund Alfa's new plant in Skokie under his Economically Targeted Investment program. Also pictured are (left) State Senator Howard Carroll (D-Chicago) and Younus Suleman (right), Quinn's liaison to the Asian-American community. The prosperity of the immigrants often led to opportunities for establishing political connections and expanding business. (Courtesy of *India Tribune*.)

Chitra Ragavan joined John Calloway's *Chicago Tonight* in 1984 and became the first Asian Indian on-air TV reporter in a major market. After 8 years at WTTW, she went on to become the first Asian Indian reporter on National Public Radio. (Courtesy of WTTW.)

Ramesh Goyal (second from left) celebrates with his mother (center) and other family members at the September 2002 opening in Highland Park of his 12th Dunkin' Donuts store. Indian-owned fast food restaurants, convenience stores, and motel franchises not only provided employment for relatives and newcomers but also turned faltering outlets into profitable ventures, leading corporations to seek out other franchisees from the Indian community. (Photo by Mukul Roy.)

Pramod Shah (right), owner of Nisha Auto Body and Mechanical Shop in Chicago, talks to customers at his store. Indian entrepreneurs established small business enterprises in a wide variety of fields. (Courtesy of Pramod Shah.)

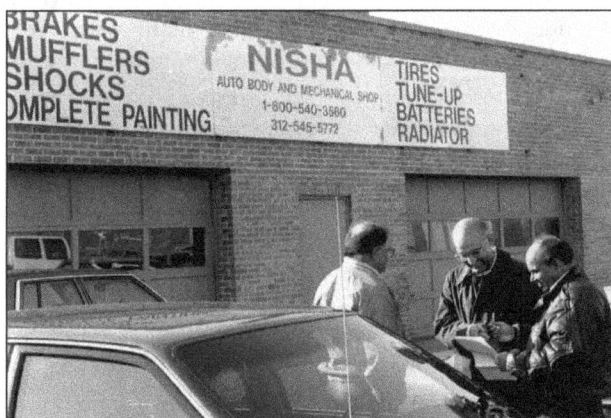

Hasan Merchant (center) founder and CEO of the Polo Group stands with his staff outside his downtown Marine Drive condominium conversion project, the Polo Tower. Merchant, a graduate of the Illinois Institute of Technology, formed his own construction company in 1986 after working at the engineering firm of Sargent and Lundy for five years. Indian-owned businesses thrive on referrals from within the community, but many also have strong client bases in the wider society. (Courtesy of Polo Builders.)

A woman prepares *dosai*, a popular South Indian lentil crepe at a storefront restaurant on Devon Avenue. Scores of workers, including many who were undocumented, found employment at businesses catering to the immigrant community's needs, worked grueling hours, and paved the way for a better life for their children. (Photo by Mukul Roy.)

Newsstand vendors operate a booth near Chicago's Union Station in 1990. Until the immigration boom of the 1980s when established immigrants sponsored relatives, Indians were rarely seen in unskilled occupations. Later arrivals were able to access networks established by their pioneering predecessors and found employment in the mainstream arena as tollbooth attendants, hotel workers, and taxi drivers. (Photo by Mukul Roy.)

Subhash Tailor, one of the first Indian tailoring shops on Devon Avenue, opened for business on May 20, 1986. Subhash Arora's wife Svarna (seated, left) adjusts Raj Wadhwa's *churidar* (leggings) that accompany the tunics traditional in northern India as Rahana Mahmoud and Svarna's daughters Priti and Tarun look on. As the community grew, families found opportunities to earn a living offering specialized Indian services such as tailoring, catering, and bridal makeup to the original immigrants as well as to their children for whom the allure of fine fabrics, intricate embroidery, and custom-fitted garments hold a special appeal. (Photo by Mukul Roy.)

As mainstream real estate and insurance agencies and investment brokerage houses realized the potential in marketing to Asian Indians, they employed large numbers of Indians such as Shimmi Chandra (left) who were fluent in English as well as one or more Indian languages. Other immigrants worked in niche markets within the community as travel agents and social service providers. (Courtesy of Shimmi Chandra.)

Membership Award

Presented to

Shimmi Chandra

for 10 continuous years of membership in the
DuPage Association of REALTORS®

on the 5th day of June 1992

Marge Devin
President

Ronald Lee
Executive Vice President

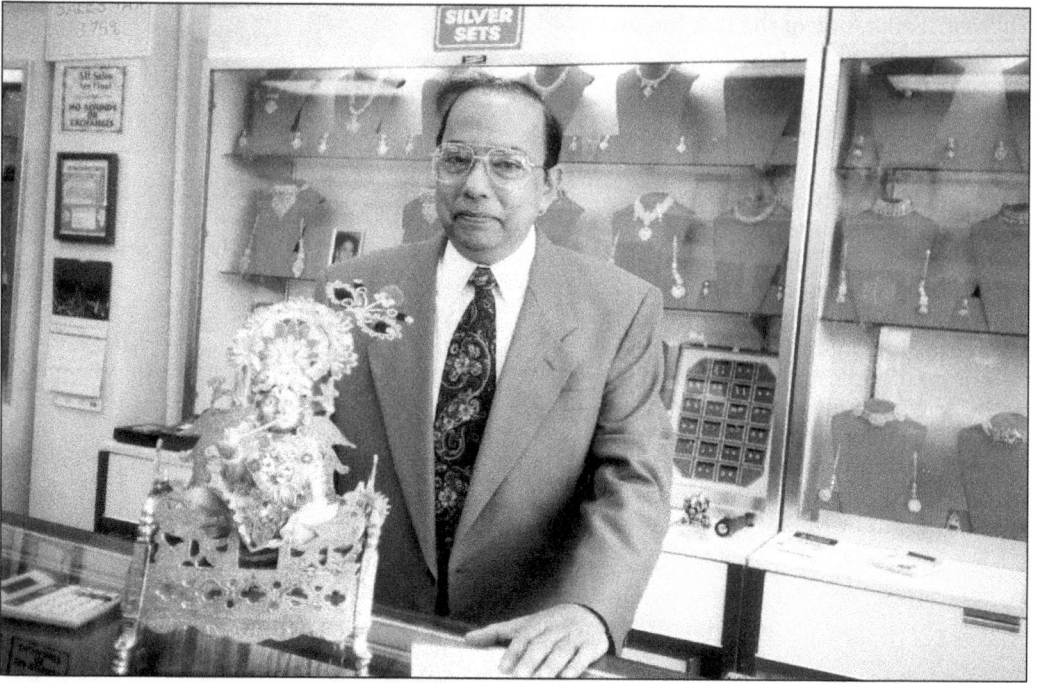

At his store, Meena Jewelers on Devon Avenue, Mahendarbhai Chatwani displays an image of Lord Krishna meant for a shrine in the home. Family-owned enterprises provided employment to dependents of the earlier immigrants who, in keeping with their cultural traditions, typically financed and supported the later arrivals until they were established on their own. (Courtesy of the Indo-American Center.)

Kannan Bhattacharya, a priest at the Sri Venkateswara Temple in Aurora, is one of many priests and chefs from India who arrived in Chicago under special visa provisions because their unique skills and training were not available in the United States. (Courtesy of *India Tribune*.)

Officer Tomi Methipara of the 24th Police District–Rogers Park joined the Chicago Police Department as its first Indian police officer in 1980 and worked as a beat officer for five years before joining the Community Policing Office. His assignment to the Devon area is a sign of the Chicago Police Department's increasing awareness of the need for members of the city's ethnic populations on its police force. (Photo by Mukul Roy.)

Bilingual, general, and special education teachers of Indian origin at Alessandro Volta Elementary School in Chicago in 2002 (left to right) Dipal Parekh, Saduqa Ahmad, Naseem Umar, Nirmala Parikh, Tahniath Masood, and Sakina Sabeeh reflect the increasing presence of Indian students in Chicago schools. By 2001, Volta School had the city's largest Gujarati student population and the school's Local School Council had the city's largest percentage of Indian members. (Courtesy of Naseem Umar.)

Dipak Jain (front row, holding book), Dean of Northwestern University's Kellogg School of Management, stands next to Professor and Mrs. Bala Balachandran, students, and participants at the university's annual India Business Club seminar in 2002. Dipak Jain is the first Asian Indian dean of a leading business school, continuing a tradition of Indian scholars at top levels in management studies in the U.S. (Photo by Mukul Roy.)

Rajat Gupta, managing director of McKinsey and Company, joined the management consultancy firm following his graduation from the Harvard School of Business in 1973 and came to live in Chicago in 1986. In 1994, he became the first Indian-born CEO to head a U.S. transglobal firm. (Courtesy of Indo-American Center.)

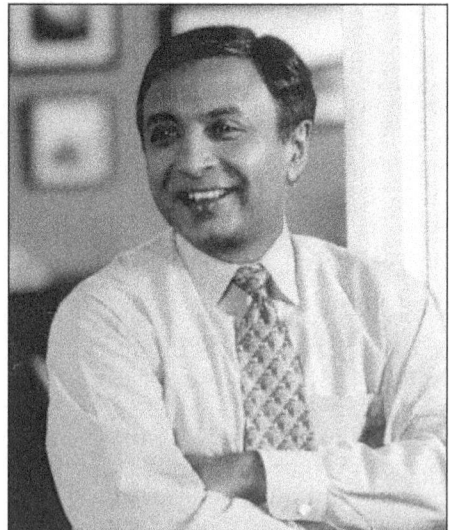

Rono Dutta became president of Elk Grove-based United Airlines in July 1999, the second Indian at the head of an American airline. (Rakesh Gangwal of U.S. Airways was the first.) Senior management positions in several other industrial and management consultancy corporations in Chicago are held by Asian Indians. (Courtesy of Indo-American Center.)

Members of the Indian Cultural Association at Lucent Technologies were enthusiastic participants in the August 17, 2002 Indian Independence Day parade on Devon Avenue. Chicago-area companies such as Lucent Technologies, Bell Labs, and Motorola employed large numbers of Indians to meet the demands of the booming high-tech industry. (Courtesy of Hemant Patel.)

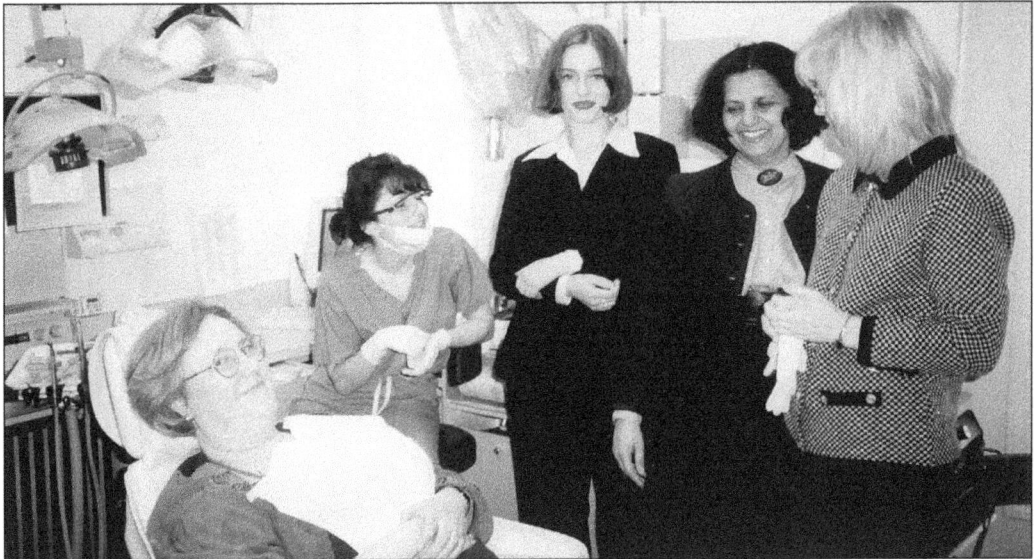

Mridu Sekhar (fourth from left), management consultant, Sidvim, Inc., oversees the first clinical session conducted in 1995 by her company which exports state of-the-art American dental technology to Russia and plans a similar venture in India. With their professional training, international network of family and friends, and linguistic abilities, Indians were uniquely positioned to participate in the global economy brought about by technological advances. Many Indian-born Chicago area residents established or found employment in companies working on projects in various parts of the world. (Courtesy of Mridu Sekhar.)

Sujata Somani relaxes in the staff lounge at the University of Chicago Medical School in 1986 during her residency in Obstetrics and Gynecology. Many offspring of Indians who immigrated in the 1960s and 70s have followed their elders into careers in medicine. (Photo by Mukul Roy.)

(Left to right) Binal Patel, Veena Jain, Asheesh Agarwal, Ashish Prasad, Chief Judge Marvin Aspen of the Northern District of Illinois, Rena Van Tine, Sanjay Tailor, Rohit Sahgal, and Deepak Sathy gather at the Indian-American Bar Association inaugural event, held on September 13, 2000. While a large number of second generation Indians chose to go into medicine, many have entered fields less traditionally chosen by Indians in Chicago, such as law, education, and music. (Courtesy of Rena Van Tine.)

Three

FAMILY LIFE
PRESERVATION AND ADAPTATION

Families are the center of life in the Asian Indian community. When Asian Indians arrived in Chicago in the 1950s and 60s, they looked to their fellow Indian students and colleagues to fill the aching void caused by separation from their families. They gathered together to celebrate each other's birthdays, religious events, and holiday festivities. International phone calls were prohibitively expensive, travel to India was out of the question, and long letters to and from home were read, re-read, and cherished. As communication improved and travel became easier, members of extended families joined early immigrants, children married and had children of their own, and immigrants began to savor the sense of well being and security that comes from being with their own kin. The availability of foodstuffs and accoutrements associated with family events made it possible to conduct observances in accordance with customs and practices in India. However, practical constraints of living in a climate and a country far removed from the origins of these practices, desire to participate fully in American society, and marriage to non-Indians served to make the family's sense of its Indian identity less pronounced. Nonetheless, strong family connections thrive, and travel to India to visit relatives and splendors of the land-of-origin continue to nurture ethnic pride in Indian heritage.

Family members assemble for a photo following a 2000 reunion at Gaylord India, a restaurant in suburban Schaumburg. Dr. Kamal Chawla (front left) arrived with his wife Urmilla (in white sari) in 1967 and paved the way for numerous relatives to follow. (Courtesy of Urmilla Chawla.)

As in their homeland, social events among immigrants from India include the entire family. Young Indian American women (left to right) Leena (Gupta) Patel with her son Shaan, Sridevi Chawla with son Amar and baby girl Arya, and Sunaina Sahgal with niece Savina Sahgal pose at a 2001 luncheon party. (Courtesy of Urmilla Chawla.)

Ranjini and Priya Rajan enjoy fast food, Indian style, at the Skokie home of their grandmother Chitra while their Uncle Krishnan looks on. Strong family ties continue to prevail among immigrant Indians. (Courtesy of R.S. Rajan.)

Asian Indians in Chicago celebrate many life events in the traditional manner. A few days before the marriage of Chinar Shah (seated right), the bride's mother and friends perform *Grah Shanti* by filling a new clay pot called *Ganesh Matali* with water from a nearby lake and carrying it in a procession for *puja* (worship) to assure marital harmony. (Courtesy of Panna Sheth.)

Roger Playle kneels before his garlanded bride, Priya Rangaswamy, to guide her footsteps during their marriage ceremony in 1999 at the Ashton Place Banquet Hall in Willowbrook. Often marriage between an Asian Indian and a non-Indian is celebrated with traditional Indian rituals. (Courtesy of Padma Rangaswamy.)

Meena Pandey and Sanjiv Bhatia are greeted with an *arati* (devotional circling of wick and flame arranged on a platter) at the bride's Burr Ridge home after their wedding in 1992. In a traditional combined family, the newlyweds move into the husband's parents' home, but in the U.S. most young couples live on their own. (Photo by Mukul Roy.)

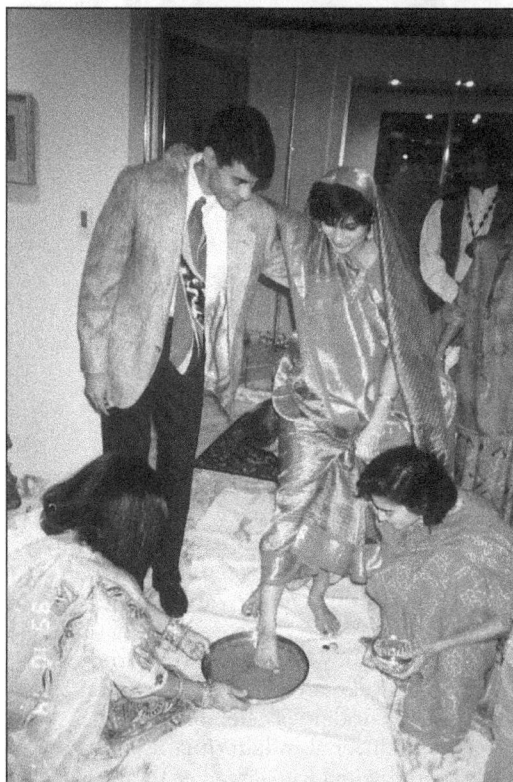

Rahil Bandukwala helps his sister, Shabnum Sanghvi, mark a path with footprints to indicate family love, support, and guidance for her child during a 1995 *Khola Bharva* at the Glenview home of Manoj and Shobana Sanghvi. Family and friends fill the lap of the mother-to-be with tokens of good wishes for her child during this ceremony in the seventh month of pregnancy. (Courtesy of Shobhana Sanghvi.)

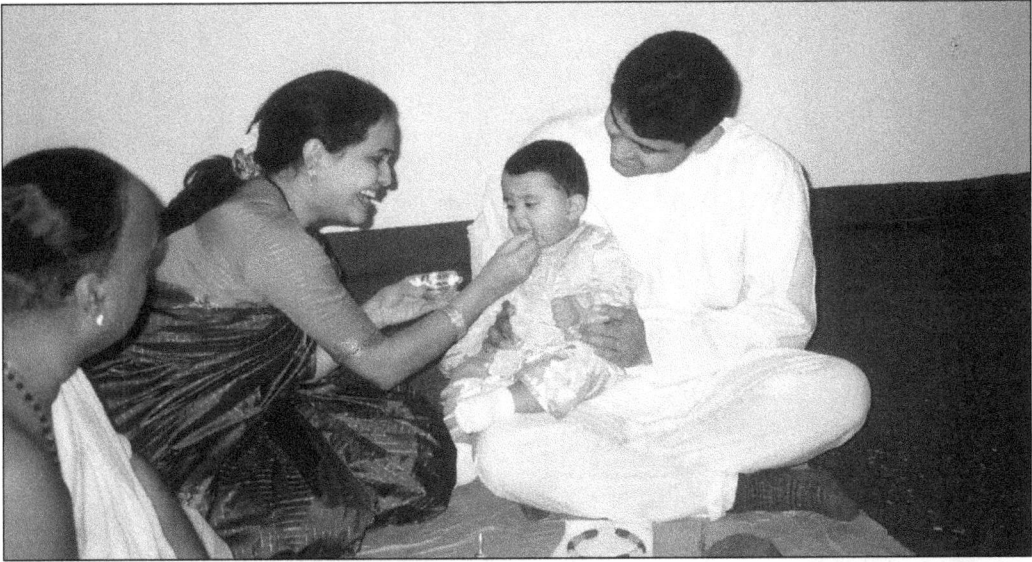

Baby Amar is fed rice for the first time by his parents, Sridevi and Anshuman Chawla, during his 1998 *annaprasana* ceremony performed by a priest at the Hindu Temple of Chicago in Lemont. (Courtesy of Urmilla Chawla.)

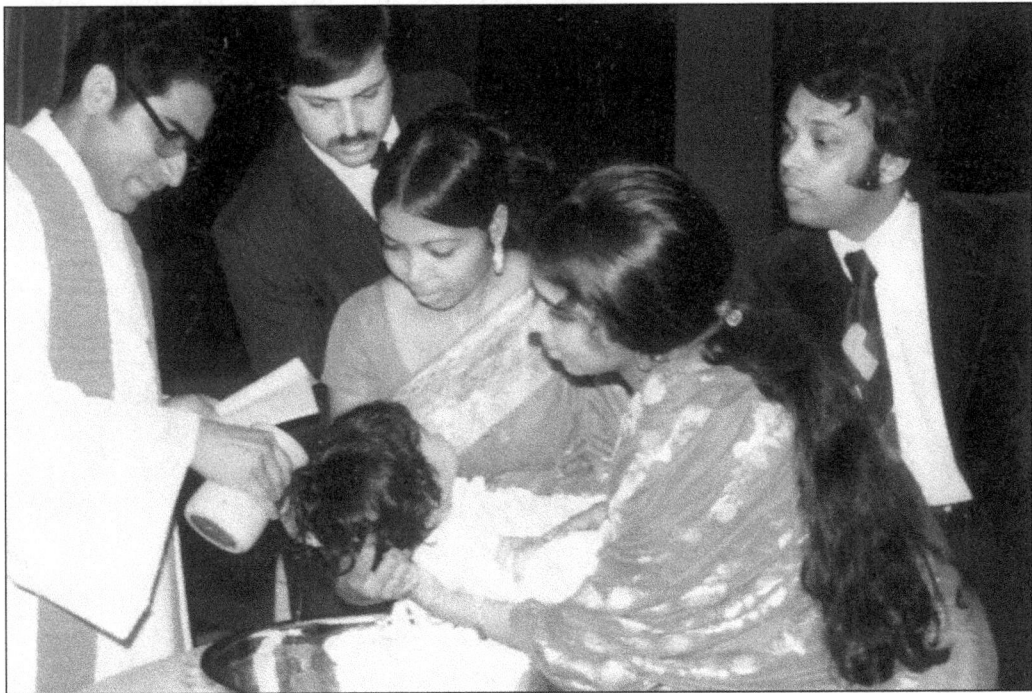

Baby Nisha, held by her mother Teresa, is baptized by a priest while her godparents, Larry and Daisy Spanier, and her father John Chirayil (right) of Glenview look on. Parents and godparents promise to provide religious instruction and guidance for the child who is dedicated to Christ during the sacrament of baptism. Christians comprise a significant portion of the Asian Indian population in the Chicago area where numerous congregations conduct services in regional languages including Hindi, Malayalam, Tamil, and Telegu. (Courtesy of John Chirayil.)

Parents Zohra and Waseem Khadir of Wheeling sit with four-year-old twins, Saif Abdul and Sheeba, during a *Bismilla* Ceremony held in Hyderabad, India in 1997. The Imam recites "I begin in the name of Allah, who is very kind and merciful" and each child repeats a few verses from the *Quran*. Relatives and friends crown the children with flowers and the parents distribute *ladoos* (sweets) to guests to celebrate the children's reaching an age of discernment. (Courtesy of Dr. Mohammed Mandur.)

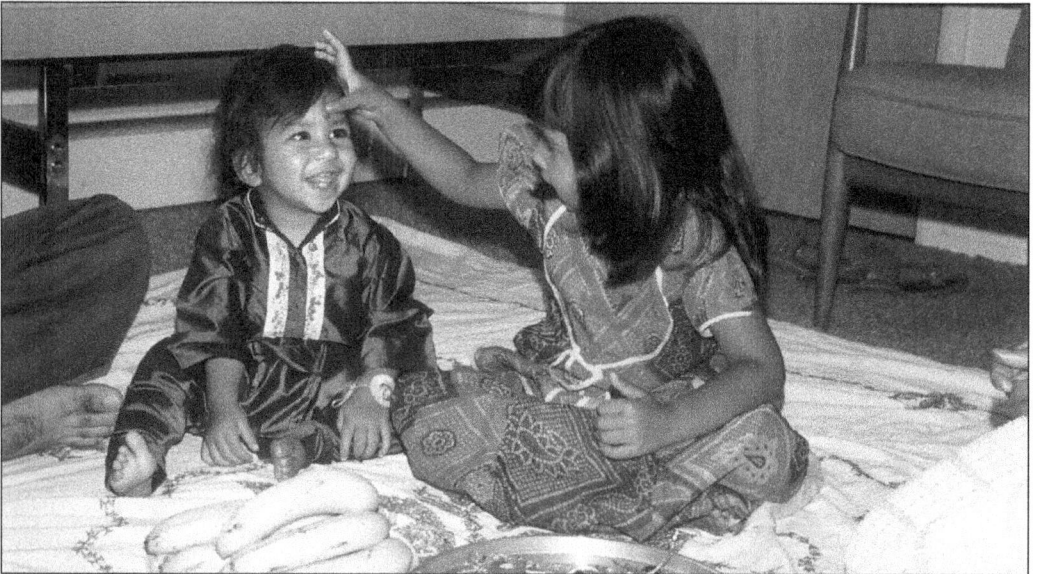

Stasha Jain of Oak Park marks her brother Neil's forehead with vermilion powder after tying a *rakhi* (bracelet) on his wrist in 1975. This ceremony assures protection of sister by brother. According to legend the annual *Raksha Bandhan* festival originated when a Rajput princess sent a *rakhi* to a Mughal emperor after she was threatened by invaders. He immediately sent aid to protect her kingdom. (Courtesy of Rani Jain.)

Joined by a Hindu priest, friends, and their daughters at their Oak Park home in 1974, Gyan and Sadhna Agarwal observe *Divali*, the Hindu festival of lights celebrating the triumph of good over evil and invoking blessings of Lakshmi, goddess of prosperity. The joyous festival of *Divali* occurs on the night of the new moon in *Kartik* (late October or early November). After worship, there is a feast and people celebrate throughout the night with games of chance and fireworks. Chicago area Hindus observe *Divali* at area temples and illuminate their homes with Christmas lights in lieu of *diyas* (tiny oil lamps) traditionally used in India. (Courtesy of Gyan Agarwal.)

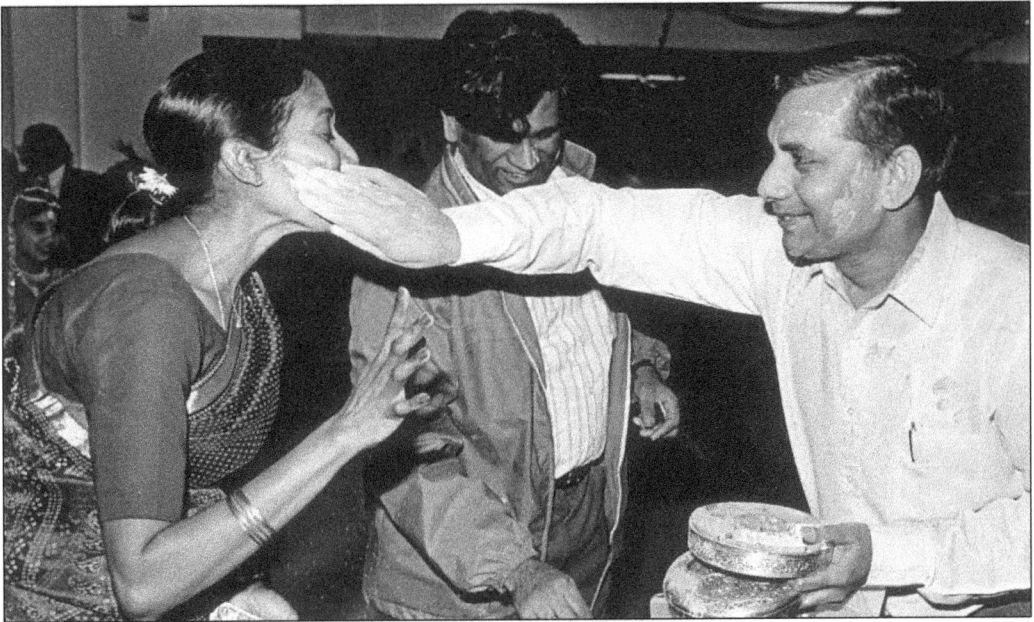

During the spring festival of *Holi*, everyone rejoices upon the return of color to the landscape and enjoys merrymaking as the *gopis* (milkmaids) did with their beloved Lord Krishna. Celebrants spray each other with colored water in a gala "water fight" or smear colored powder as these revelers did at the Ganesh Temple in Lemont in 1995. (Photo by Mukul Roy.)

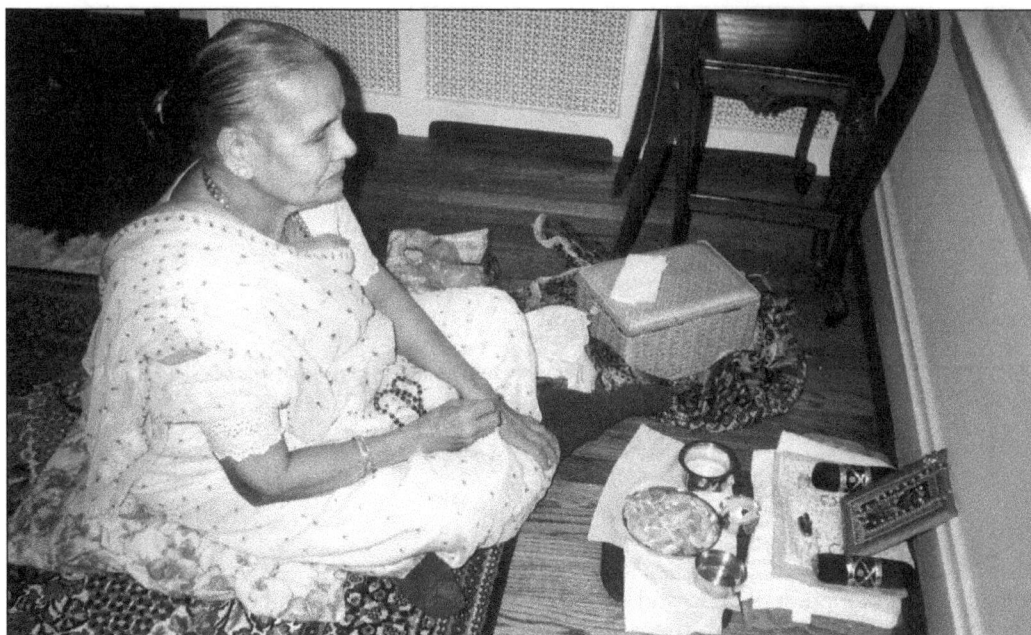

Like thousands of devout Hindus, Maniben P. Shah invokes blessings for members of her household and offers *prasad* (fresh fruit and warm sweetened milk) to her household deity during daily *puja* (devotions) at her son's home in Evanston in 1989. (Courtesy of Dorothie Shah.)

Supervised by a priest, Manotosh Banerji participates in the 1986 *Upanayana* of his son Ranjan while the boy's mother, Basanti, looks on. For this occasion their River Forest home was decorated with an auspicious *rangoli* design of symbols intended to bring harmony and protection to the household. *Upanayana*, the rite of initiation and investiture with the sacred thread, symbol of high caste worn over the left shoulder, is an important event in the life of a Hindu Brahmin male. (Photo by Mukul Roy.)

Carving Thanksgiving turkey is a cooperative endeavor managed by surgeon, Dr. Umesh Sharma (right) under the watchful eyes of friends Dr. Ram Pankaj (left) and Dr. Virendra Bisla (center). The traditional Thanksgiving menu is usually more appreciated by the second generation and is often accompanied by typical Indian dishes enjoyed by their parents, many of whom are vegetarians. (Courtesy of Urmilla Chawla.)

Family members gather in front of the India Catholic Association of America tree at the 1998 Museum of Science and Industry Christmas Around the World Festival. Christmas festivities are enjoyed by both Christian and non-Christian Asian Indians. (Courtesy of Hector Lobo.)

New Year's Eve of the new millennium prompted frolicking with friends. Indian immigrants celebrated the arrival of the New Year in homes and in Indian restaurants which featured entertainment and dancing to popular Indian music for the occasion. (Photo courtesy of Mukul Roy.)

Relatives from the homeland often arrive in Chicago in time for major milestones in the immigrant family's life. Rahul Sekhar's 1988 High School graduation was an occasion for smiles with proud grandparents Mr. and Mrs. V.C. Dore, who were visiting from India. (Courtesy of Mridu Sekhar.)

Great grand-children eagerly anticipate a slice of cake at the celebration of Amarnath Sharma's eighty-eighth birthday in 1984. (Courtesy of Prem Sharma.)

Forming a pyramid of cousins is a gala highlight of a family gathering. (Courtesy of Urmilla Chawla.)

Four

RELIGION

KEEPING THE FAITH

Indians are a deeply religious people, and the immigrant community in Chicago reflects the religious diversity of the homeland with adherents of the Hindu, Muslim, Sikh, Christian, Jain, Zoroastrian, and Jewish faiths. There is no official count of the religious affiliation of immigrant groups but it is estimated that more than 80 percent of Chicago's Indian immigrant population is Hindu, reflecting roughly the same proportion as in the homeland.

Beginning in the 1960s and 70s, Hindus worshiped in homes under a broad Hindu identity, but as their numbers grew in the following decades, they regrouped according to narrower preferences. The result is a proliferation of temples dedicated to different deities in the Hindu pantheon.

The remarkable organizational and fund-raising skills of the professional and economically successful elite enabled them to build several religious structures, each worth millions of dollars, in the short span of thirty years. Temples, mosques, *gurudwaras* (Sikh houses of worship), and churches are not only places of worship, but centers of social and cultural activity where new generations of Indians, born and brought up in Chicago, meet to carry on their traditions.

Indian immigrants have made many adjustments to American conditions. A religious holiday that might fall in the middle of the week is often celebrated on weekends when visits to the temple are easier. Volunteers at religious institutions participate in mainstream society through involvement in charitable work, such as soup kitchens and food pantries at Thanksgiving and Christmas.

The Hindu Temple of Greater Chicago, or Sri Rama Temple in Lemont, is the oldest Hindu temple built by Indian immigrants in the Chicago area. The foundation stone for the temple was laid on June 17, 1984 by N.T. Rama Rao, Chief Minister of Andhra Pradesh. The *Kumbhabhishekam* or inauguration of Sri Rama Temple was celebrated between June 27 and July 6, 1986, with full religious ceremonies. The temple complex includes a large community center with banquet hall and auditorium for social, cultural, and religious events. (Photo by Urmilla Chawla.)

Professionals from the entire Chicagoland area have provided leadership of the Hindu Temple of Greater Chicago. The Board of Directors in 1990-91 is pictured from left to right, (seated) Madhav Reddy, Harinath Bathina, Amrish Mahajan, Upendranath Nimmagadda, Ashutosh Gupta, Krishna Reddy, Kamal Chawla, and Muni Ratnam; (standing) Durga Chanduri, Marella Hanumadass, B. Ramachandran, Vichitra Nayyar, Vijay Dave, Bansi Sharma, Bosebabu Mandava, Urmilla Chawla, and Krishnappa. (Courtesy of Urmilla Chawla.)

In 1986, the *Prathishtapana* or installation of deity was performed at the Rama Temple. The same year saw the *shilpis* (sculptors) from India work long hours to carve the intricate *gopuram* (temple tower) that eventually covered the bare cement exterior of the Rama temple seen in the background. (Photo by Urmilla Chawla.)

44

The main altar at the Hindu Temple includes images of Lord Rama, his wife Sita, and brother Lakshmana, whose story is told in the epic *Ramayana*. The website of the Hindu Temple emphasizes that Hindus are not worshipping idols but aspects of the divinity that they represent. (Photo by B.S. Subbakrishna.)

The Vishwa Hindu Parishad of America held its Second Annual Youth Conference in Chicago in 1992. The VHP has strong political connections to the ruling Bhartiya Janata Party in India, but not all Chicago Hindus approve of the mix of politics and religion. Hindu Student Councils, created to help keep university students educated and interested in Hinduism, are active on campuses in the Chicago area.

Vishwa Hindu Parishad Of America, Inc.
Greater Chicago Chapter

The Second Annual Hindu Youth Conference
August 1, 1992

HINDU YOUTH
GROWING UP IN AMERICA

'Ask nothing; want nothing in return. Give what you have to give; it will come back to you - but do not think of that now. It will come back multiplied.. You have the power to give. Give, and there it ends.'

— SWAMI VIVEKANANDA

VISION
2000

Various aspects of Hinduism are reflected in the different structures throughout the Chicago area. Ganesh Temple in Lemont, part of the Hindu Temple of Greater Chicago, was built in the Kalinga style and houses the shrines of Siva, Parvati, Ganesha, Durga and Subramaniaswamy. It is one of many magnificent temple structures that form part of Chicago's religious landscape. (Photo by Urmilla Chawla.)

The Shri Swaminarayan Temple in Wheeling (pictured here) and another Swaminarayan Temple in Itasca are part of the network of such temples around the world. (Courtesy of *India Tribune*.)

Bochasanwasi Shri Akshar Purushottam Swaminarayan Sanstha (BAPS) Temple in Bartlett is one of more than 450 temples and 6,000 centers spread across 45 countries around the globe. The Chinmaya Mission in Hinsdale and the Hari Om Mandir in Medinah are among other area institutions devoted to the Hindu religion. (Photo by B.S. Subbakrishna.)

The Sri Venkateswara (Balaji) Temple in Aurora is built in a South Indian style and caters to an orthodox South Indian population. Located farther west than the Rama Temple, it draws worshippers from as far away as Rockford and Minnesota. (Photo by Mukul Roy.)

Water from holy rivers of India is poured on images as they are installed in a 48-day *puja* (worship service) during *Kumbabhisekham* or inauguration ceremonies for the Balaji temple in Aurora in 1985. (Photo by Mukul Roy.)

Chicago's Hindu institutions have adopted American ways in order to raise money for worthy causes and participate in mainstream society. A 2000 walkathon, led by saffron-robed swamis or holy men of the BAPS Temple, is an example. (Courtesy of *India Tribune*.)

Devotees pray around a fire as a female priest, Kusum Patel (fourth from right), performs a *yagna* or ritual ceremony attended by several thousands in the parking lot of Soldier Field in 1995. Sponsored by Gayatri Pariwar of Chicago, an organization with followers in 100 countries, such *yagnas* include the chanting of Vedic *mantras* and are performed simultaneously in many parts of the world with prayers for peace and harmony. (Courtesy of *India Tribune*.)

48

Brinda Bijawat (left, kneeling) observes
Mahasivratri (The Great Night of Siva)
along with family and friends in her
Naperville home in March 2002 with a *puja*
(worship) to create, in her words, "good
vibrations." Hindus observe the occasion
both as a discipline and a festivity, keeping
a strict fast and all-night vigil, meditating,
and singing *bhajans* (hymns) in praise of
Lord Siva. (Photo by Sanjay Bijawat.)

The International Society for Krishna
Consciousness (ISKCON) sponsors the
annual *Jagannatha Ratha Yatra* procession,
where a 40-foot tall chariot bearing the
images of Hindu deities is drawn down
Devon Avenue. The event culminates
in a festival of music, plays, and dance
at Warren Park on Western Avenue.
(Courtesy of *India Tribune*.)

An altar for Mahavira, the founder of the Jain religion which advocates peace and non-violence, was created at the 11th Biennial JAINA convention at the Rosemont Convention Center in 2001. JAINA is a Federation of the Jain Societies of North America and includes the Jain Society of Metropolitan Chicago which was established in 1969. Indian Jains, many of whom belong to the prosperous business community, come from all over the world, including Africa and Fiji. They are strict vegetarians. Their magnificent Jain temple in Bartlett was inaugurated in 1993. (Courtesy of *India Tribune*.)

Representatives of the Jain religious community from around the world gather outside The Palmer House for the 1993 World's Parliament of Religions. In keeping with their non-violent and religious practices, Jain priests and nuns mask their mouths in order to avoid ingesting any living organisms. (Photo by Mukul Roy.)

Indian Muslims worship jointly with Muslims of other nationalities in Donnelly Hall at McCormick Place in 2002 on *Eid-ul-Fitr*, the feast day that concludes *Ramadan*, the annual month of fasting. (Photo by Mukul Roy.)

The Burhani Park Masjid in Hinsdale, one of the largest mosques in North America (30,000 square feet), was built in 2001 for the 1,000-strong Dawoodi Bohra Muslim community of Chicago at a cost of $9 million. It has 104 chandeliers and ancient wooden pillars brought from Surat, India. Its traditional Islamic architecture follows the middle eastern Fatimid style and was designed to blend with modern western styles. (Courtesy of Polo Builders.)

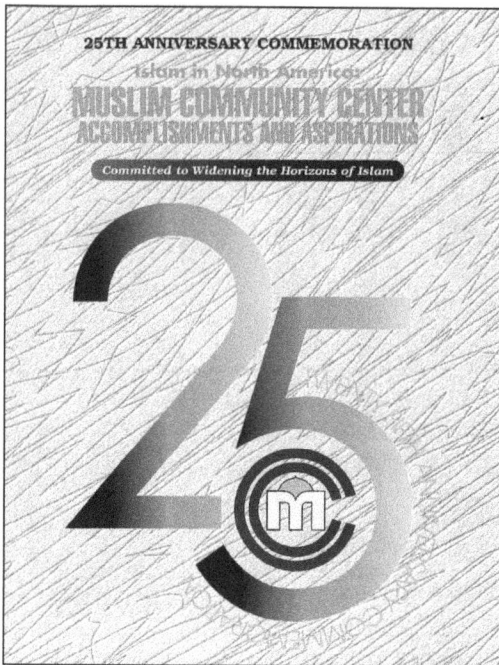

The Muslim Community Center's 25th anniversary souvenir, published in 1995, celebrates the community's achievements. The Muslim religious community runs full time schools in several Chicago locations, including Villa Park, Lombard, and Bridgeview, where Islamic studies and Arabic language studies are taught along with regular state required courses. (Courtesy of Muslim Community Center.)

Second grader Samiya Rahman and her classmates in Morton Grove, Illinois can choose from many more study and reading resources than American-born, English-speaking Muslim children could do just a few years ago. Samiya holds one of some 100 titles published by the Iqra' International Educational Foundation of Skokie, which was established in 1983 to provide children with materials that facilitate understanding of their Islamic religious heritage. (Courtesy of Iqra' International Educational Foundation of Skokie.)

The Sikh Religious Society of Chicago built a contemporary *gurudwara* for worship in Palatine in the 1970s in keeping with their religion, which emphasizes the simple, service-oriented life. The Sikh religion was founded in the 15th century in India and incorporates the teachings of Hinduism and Islam. (Photo B.S. Subbakrishna.)

The singing of *kirtans* or devotional songs as a form of prayer is fostered at an early age among Sikh youth. Observant Sikhs do not cut their hair. Young boys cover their topknots with *putkas* while adult males wear turbans. (Courtesy of Punjabi Cultural Society.)

On March 31, 2001, Pope John Paul II announced the creation of a new diocese for the 100,000 Syro-Malabar Catholics of the United States and Canada. Mar Jacob Angadiath, director of the Syro-Malabar in Chicago was ordained as the first bishop of this new diocese on July 1, 2001. The Episcopal consecration, held in Chicago during the second Syro-Malabar Catholic Convention of North America, was attended by Mar Kuriakose Kunnachery, Bishop of Kottayam, Cardinal Varkey Vithayathil, Head of the Syro-Malabar Catholic Church (center), and Vatican Representative His Grace Gabriel Montalvo, Epistolic Nuncio to the U.S. Christianity in India began with the apostle St. Thomas who is said to have traveled to Kerala and preached the gospel there. (Courtesy of *India Tribune*.)

Indian nuns from the Franciscan Clarist Congregation of Minneapolis converse with Cardinal Varkey Vithayathil during the 2001 national convention in Chicago. The Catholic commitment to charity also prompted the establishment of a Chicago branch of Mother Teresa's order, the Missionaries of Charity. Nuns from Mother Teresa's order in Kolkata (Calcutta) came to staff the mission at St. Malachy's on the near west side and minister to inner city residents. (Photo by Mukul Roy.)

54

A young Indian from the India Catholic Association of America greets Joseph Cardinal Bernardin, Archbishop of Chicago at Our Lady of Victory Church, Chicago on March 6, 1994. (Courtesy of Hector Lobo.)

The India Mission Telugu United Methodist Church is one of many Protestant groups in the Indian Christian community which is very diverse, with several churches based on denominational and linguistic differences. Here, the India Mission Choir from Chicago and Oak Park is performing a traditional Telugu spiritual "Hallelujah." (Courtesy of *India Tribune*.)

Members of the Zoroastrian Association of Chicago, founded in 1975, gather outside the Zoroastrian Center of Chicago in Hinsdale. The Center was opened in 1983 and provides social, cultural, and religious services to the community. Zoroastrians are one of the smallest groups in the world, numbering only 200,000 worldwide. About 700 Parsis, as they are commonly known, reside in the Chicago area. (Courtesy of *Fezana Journal*/Roshan Rivetna.)

As they pray, young Zoroastrian priests and their elders wear *padaan* (masks) to avoid contaminating the sacred fire in the temple. Zoroastrians venerate all light and fire as symbols of God's creation. (Courtesy of *Fezana Journal*/Roshan Rivetna.)

Five

DEVON AVENUE
ETHNIC MARKETPLACE

Not until the 1980s did the Indian business district along Devon Avenue become a noticeable presence on the Chicago scene, offering the immigrants an ethnic enclave where they could satisfy their longings for food, entertainment, and products from their homeland.

Many of the early Indian immigrants had initially settled in the Rogers Park area, attracted by its ethnic diversity, affordable housing, and accessible transportation. A few Greek, Russian, and Assyrian stores, harbingers of the "International Marketplace" to come, had already appeared in the declining Jewish business district when two Indian stores opened on Devon Avenue during the early 1970s. Before long, the area was teeming with activity again, fueled by the availability of low cost retail spaces, the entrepreneurial energy of the immigrants who arrived in the 1980s, and the financial backing of their now prosperous forebears. By the end of the 1990s, merchants claimed that the area was the largest Indian shopping district in North America, and Chicagoans had come to think of this portion of the street as "Little India."

The Devon community, with its family-owned businesses, hardships, and success stories represents a significant aspect of Chicago's Indian immigrant story.

Large crowds along Devon Avenue enjoy the August 1994 annual Indian Independence Day parade. Originally held on Michigan Avenue, it featured the mayor and other politicians as chief guests. A shift to a more ethnic composition accompanied the shift in venue, and celebrities from India appeared as guests of honor. By the end of the 1980s, rivalry between organizations vying for the privilege of representing the community had subsided, and the Federation of India Associations became the official parade organizers. (Photo by Mukul Roy.)

Managers Nari Nagrani (left) and Ratan Sharma take a break during the May 1973 opening of India Sari Palace (ISP), the first Indian sari store on the street. Fabrics in the store included six-yard lengths of printed French chiffon for $40 and synthetics from Japan for $10.50 to $19.50. Many businesses on Devon are branches of enterprises owned by members of the Indian diaspora located in other parts of the world. ISP is a branch of a family business owned by Indians who settled in Hong Kong in the 1940s. The parent company chose the 2538 W. Devon Avenue location based on the north side addresses in their mail order customer list. (Courtesy of Ratan Sharma.)

As demand for Japanese synthetic fabrics fell, India Sari Palace expanded into the restaurant and real estate arenas by reducing the size of the sari shop in 1995 to open Tiffin, one of the more upscale restaurants on Devon Avenue. (Photo by Urmilla Chawla.)

Shoppers from all over the Midwest stock their pantries at Patel Brothers located at 2610 W. Devon Avenue. This family business conglomerate sprang from humble beginnings in 1974 with a tiny grocery store at the corner of Devon Avenue and Hoyne. It leased space from India Sari Palace in 1978 to be closer to what became the heart of the Indian business district and then added this more spacious location. (Photo by Urmilla Chawla.)

By the new millennium, the remodeled Patel Brothers grocery store had changed the look of the block with the first "Indianized" façade on Devon Avenue. The Patel empire had grown to include restaurants, appliance stores, travel agencies, satellite network services, and large sections of real estate. (Photo by B.S. Subbakrishna.)

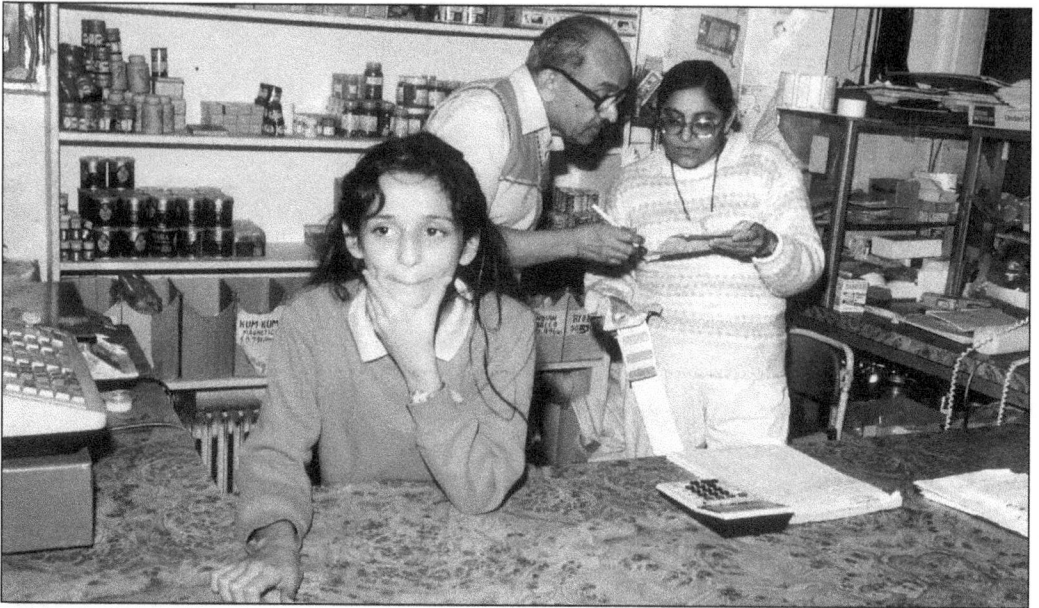

Mrs. Aruna Patel (right) looks over store receipts while her daughter Susan plays at the counter. This tiny store was the foundation of the Patel business empire that extends across the United States. (Photo by Mukul Roy.)

Mafat Patel (left), affectionately known as the mayor of Devon, stands with brother Tulsi in his newly refurbished Patel Brothers grocery store in 1996. The Patel story is a typical American immigrant success story shaped by the family ties and cultural traditions of their native Gujarat. Mafat Patel came to the U.S. in 1968 to study electrical engineering. He sponsored his brother Tulsi who, with his wife Aruna, established the Patel Brothers grocery store in 1974. As the store prospered, the Patels expanded into a variety of enterprises that provided a livelihood for numerous other family members. The sons of the two brothers earned professional degrees and joined the processing and distributing ends of the family business with Swad products and Raja Foods based in Skokie. (Courtesy of *India Tribune*.)

Mr. and Mrs. Harjivan Vitha (left) arrived from Africa in 1972. Mr. Vitha operated a jewelry business from his home, and opened a store on Devon Avenue in 1981 to meet the growing demand for his products. As the community prospered, the family opened stores across the country, reportedly becoming the largest 22-karat jewelry business in the United States. The eight Vitha sons, most of whom have professional qualifications from U.S. universities, left their careers to run the eight stores. Ramesh Vitha (right) is pictured in 1996 in front of the display case in his Devon Avenue store. (Mr. and Mrs. Vitha photo by Mukul Roy. Ramesh Vitha photo courtesy of *India Tribune*.)

Visitors sample the wares at the November 1983 opening of Foods'n'Flavors. Like jewelry stores, many restaurants on Devon Avenue are family-owned enterprises. Fast food snack shops are popular spots to meet friends or take a break from shopping. (Photo by Mukul Roy.)

Sales clerk Urmila Jain pauses amidst a display of synthetic fabrics imported from Hong Kong and Singapore at Taj Sari Palace in 1983. Until the latter part of the 1980s, the merchandise in sari shops and other stores on Devon Avenue catered to immigrants purchasing gifts to take back to India where severe foreign exchange restrictions made imported fabrics and electrical items coveted luxuries. (Photo by Mukul Roy.)

Members of the second generation like Sonal Goenka and Sneh Diwan dress for wedding receptions and other special occasions in fashionable ethnic outfits such as *ghagra choli* (long skirt, short blouse and scarf) and *salwar kameez* (tunic and pants.) By the late 1980s, stores on Devon Avenue responded to a shift in the marketplace by stocking ethnic Indian merchandise including handwoven silk saris for use by Indian Americans. The *bindi* (dot) on the girls' foreheads is widely used as a cosmetic although on older women it may be an indication of marital status. (Courtesy of *India Tribune*.)

Stores such as Atlantic Video offering Indian music and films in a variety of languages help keep the immigrant population in touch with the latest in entertainment from the homeland. Attracted by the lavish costumes and dances typical of Bollywood films, the children of many Indian immigrants gain familiarity with their parents' native languages. (Courtesy of *India Tribune*.)

In March 1993 Mahesh Sharma opened a news kiosk on the corner of Devon and Rockwell Avenues where he sold periodicals in Indian regional languages as well as English language Indian publications such as *Filmfare, Femina,* and *India Today.* Following its success, he opened the first Indian book store, India Book House, at 2551 W. Devon Avenue in December 1995. In 1996, he, his wife Nirupma (left), and son Rishabh received Kiran Bedi, New Delhi's renowned police chief who signed copies of her book, *I Dare.* (Courtesy of *India Tribune*.)

In the 1990s, businesses sprang up to offer services specific to the immigrant community, such as beauty services including *mehendi* (intricate designs made from vegetable dye used to decorate women's hands and feet at weddings) and custom tailoring of ethnic garments. (Photo by B.S. Subbakrishna.)

The children of the merchants and store clerks play outside a beauty shop in the late 1980s. Like their counterparts in urban India, youngsters amuse themselves in the streets near the stores that employ their parents. (Photo by Mukul Roy.)

The Indian section of Devon Avenue throbs with vitality on summer weekends. However, by the mid 1990s, parking problems and traffic congestion began to discourage suburban Indian shoppers, particularly those in the Western suburbs where Indian restaurants and shops had opened. (Photo by Urmilla Chawla.)

In a community effort to address concerns about the appearance of the area, volunteers (from left) Ranjit Ganguly, Ann Lata Kalayil, Mihir Shah, Suvodeep Ganguly, Jaideep Ganguly, Rupal Dalal, Netta D' Souza, Ashref Hashim, Matthew Kuriakose, and Syed Ali of the Indo-American Center and the Indo-American Democratic Organization organized a "Clean and Green Day" on May 1, 1999 on Devon Avenue. (Courtesy of Indo-American Center.)

P.L. Santoshi, Consul General of India, speaks at the dedication ceremony when a section of Devon Avenue was named Gandhi *Marg* (Way) in honor of the revered Indian leader. Renaming streets in honor of immigrant heroes is one way 50th Ward Alderman Bernard Stone demonstrates his responsiveness to his multiethnic constituency. Another section of Devon Avenue was named for Mohammed Ali Jinnah in honor of the Pakistani leader. (Courtesy of Indo-American Center.)

Ranjit Ganguly (left) presents a plaque to Mayor Richard M. Daley at the Indo-American Center during the dedication of Mother Teresa Way on the Center's block of California Avenue on December 13, 1997. Mother Teresa, an Albanian who grew up in Yugoslavia, received the 1979 Nobel Peace Prize for her work among the destitute on the streets of Kolkata (Calcutta). She visited Chicago in 1986 to dedicate the new convent established by her order for its work in the inner city. (Courtesy of Indo-American Center.)

The International Society for Krishna Consciousness (ISKCON) (popularly known as the Hare Krishna movement) moved to this former Masonic Lodge on Lunt Avenue in 1980. At the time its congregation comprised non-Indian followers of the movement. By 2002, the congregation of about 8,000 members was more than 85 percent Indian. In addition to its regular services, ISKCON began to perform traditional temple-based ceremonies such as weddings and first haircuts to accommodate the religious needs of the growing number of Indians in its neighborhood. (Photo by Mukul Roy.)

Sikhs change the *nishansahib* (religious flag) above their house of worship at a ceremony in observance of their new year, *baisakhi* at the Gurudwara Sahib of Chicago at 2341 W. Devon Avenue. Established in 1995, the *gurudwara* has a capacity of 250 persons, and organized its first *baisakhi* parade in 2002. The Indian neighborhood around Devon Avenue reflects the religious diversity in the homeland with Sikh, Muslim, and Hindu congregations. (Courtesy of *India Tribune*.)

Children at the Vedic Day Care Center, 3034 W. Devon Avenue, perform a play on the birth of Jesus at their 2002 Christmas celebration. The Center operates in accordance with the principles of the Hindu scriptures, the *Vedas*. Founded in 1994, it offers early childhood education and spiritual training which promotes harmony among all cultures. (Courtesy of Vedic Day Care Center.)

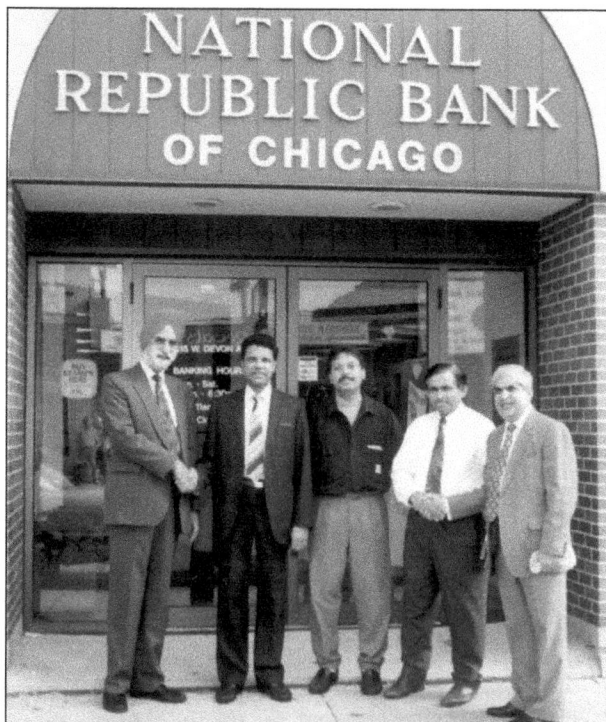

Attendees at the August 1991 opening ceremony of the Devon Avenue branch of the National Republic Bank included (left to right) Mr. Dhir of the Indian consulate, Rohit Maniar, vice-president and branch manager, Babu Patel of Sahil, Tulsi Patel of Patel Brothers, and Andy Bhatia of Air India. In 1984, a team of entrepreneurs headed by Hiren Patel and Dr. Upendranath Nimmagadda acquired the struggling National Republic Bank, making it the first Indian-owned bank in the United States. The bank has played a key role in the community, granting small loans to struggling immigrants with no credit history, assisting small businessmen to obtain franchises, and helping finance several of the community's major institutions. (Courtesy of *India Tribune*.)

Six

ARTS
TRADITION AND TRANSFORMATION

Performances of classical music and dance by leading artistes from India, commercial productions of Hindi and Gujarati plays, screenings of independent art films, and special exhibitions of visual art help strengthen traditions and inspire new forms of expression that celebrate the vibrant and varied cultural life of Chicago's Asian Indian community.

Until the mid-1970s, programs and exhibitions offered by mainstream institutions such as the Art Institute of Chicago and the Field Museum of Natural History were the primary access to India's artistic heritage for Asian Indians in Chicago. Enthusiastic audiences including Asian Indians applauded the 1967 performance by Uday Shankar and his dance company at the Auditorium Theatre and Kathakali and Manipuri dancers at the Field Museum in the 1970s and 1980s.

As their population grew, immigrants themselves organized programs, and a parallel arts scene developed within the community. *Bharata Natayam* and *Kathak* classical dance schools were established by professional dancers in their homes. Indian parents, anxious to impart to their children a vital part of their heritage, drove long distances for lessons. High school variety shows began to feature traditional dances by Indian students along with tap and ballet performances. Events staged by Indian organizations nurtured amateur talent in regional artistic traditions and grew into mega-productions featuring *raas garba* competitions and innovative fusion such as *bhangra* rap and disco *dandia* that drew participants from around the world.

Official recognition of Indian Republic Day celebrations at Daley Plaza in 1980 by Chicago Mayor Jayne Byrne included performances by young Bharata Natayam dancers. (Courtesy of Ranjit Ganguly.)

Classical sitarist Patrick Marks (center) formed the India Music Ensemble in 1973. He performed at homes and public venues throughout the Chicago area in addition to offering instruction to aspiring musicians. (Courtesy of Prem Sharma.)

The India Classical Music Society's public programs were inaugurated in 1983. Each year ICMS organizes several concerts by top-notch performers from India who perform a wide range of classical music on a variety of instruments. (Courtesy of Prem Sharma.)

South Indian classical violinist K. Subramaniam participated in the 1986 Festival of India with a concert at the Field Museum of Natural History. He has enthusiastically advocated fusion of Western and Eastern classical music. (Festival of India brochure.)

In 1985, the Chicago *Thyagaraja Utsavam* was founded "to nurture Carnatic (South Indian) music literacy" and featured regular performances by visiting musicians from India as well as local talent. (Photo by Mukul Roy.)

Manna Dey (in glasses), a popular playback singer for Indian films, performed at the home of Dr. Umesh Sharma (left) in the early 1980s. Aficionados of traditional Indian music supported visiting artistes from India by hosting soirees in their homes. (Courtesy of Prem Sharma.)

In 1982, young Sandeep Sharma, shown on the trumpet, challenged renowned santoor player Shiv Kumar Sharma: "Shivji, do you know C sharp?" By 2001, Sandeep had formed his own band, *Deep*, which performs regularly at Chicago clubs. (Courtesy of Prem Sharma.)

Sarod player Sumantra Roy pauses for a 1997 post-performance tete-a-tete with his wife, classical *Odissi* dancer, Mausumi. *Odissi* is one of several classical dance forms from India which have found proponents in the United States through instruction at schools such as Mausumi's Tribhang Dance Studio, established in 1996 in Hoffman Estates. Like many other immigrant professionals working in medicine, business, and information technology, Sumantra maintains a deep commitment to his art. (Courtesy of Mausumi Roy.)

In the time-honored tradition of Indian classical dancers, Rani Patel receives the blessing of her *guru* (teacher) Vijayalakshmi Shetty before a 1997 *Bharata Natyam* performance at Taft High School. Vijayalakshmi founded the Natraj Dance Academy in 1983. Hundreds of young dancers in the Chicago area have celebrated their *arangetrams* (dance debuts) after several years of training with performances that often feature elaborate stage arrangements and musicians from India. (Courtesy of Vijayalakshmi Shetty.)

Dancers of the Dilshad Academy perform *Kathak* at an India Tribune gala. *Kathak*, a glorious fusion of Hindu-Muslim arts from North India, is taught at area institutions including Kathak Nrityakala Kendra Academy in Elk Grove Village, established in memory of classical dancer Anila Sinha by Dr. Birendra Sinha. (Courtesy of *India Tribune*.)

In 1975, Hema Rajagopalan founded *Natyakalalayam* (temple of dance and art) to connect children of Asian Indians with their heritage through study of South India's ancient classical dance form, *Bharata Natyam*. In 1999, *Natyakalalayam* became the first U.S. based Indian dance company to perform at the Kennedy Center for the Performing Arts in Washington D.C. (Courtesy of *Natyakalalayam*.)

Krithika Rajagopalan (center), daughter of *Natyakalalayam's* founder and the company's assistant artistic director, performs with dancers at the 1995 premiere of *Shakti Chakra* (Energy Cycle) held at the College of DuPage to celebrate the school's 25th anniversary. The company was renamed *Natya Dance Theatre* to reflect its broadened vision when it transformed traditional solo performances into ensemble dance dramas to celebrate universal themes. Troupe members (clockwise from center) are Krithika Rajagopalan, Shama Patari, Deepa Rangachari, Sita Srinivasan, Reshma Chakravarthy, Maya Ramdas, Divya Sundar, Rekha Rangachari, and Nitya Sundar. (Courtesy of *Natya Dance Theatre*.)

A *Raas-Garba* dance troupe holds aloft its trophy after winning a dance competition. The Chicago area hosts many such events featuring dancers from abroad as well as throughout the U.S. *Raas-Garba* is popular among Gujaratis, especially during *Navaratri*, the nine days before *Divali*, the festival of lights, which occurs in the fall. Often an evening of *Raas* and *Dandia* (Gujarati folk dance) is scheduled the night before a wedding. (Photo by Mukul Roy.)

Indian regional organizations celebrate their heritage with dance and performances that provide opportunities for widespread participation. The cross-over success of the rousing Punjabi *Bhangra* has made it a rage in discos and dance clubs where it blends with Caribbean rhythms and rap beats. (Courtesy of Punjabi Cultural Society.)

A group of women perform *Kai Kottu Kali* at a meeting of the Malayalee Association of Chicago. A wide array of folk and classical Indian dance traditions are enjoyed at events in the Chicago area. (Courtesy of Prem Sharma.)

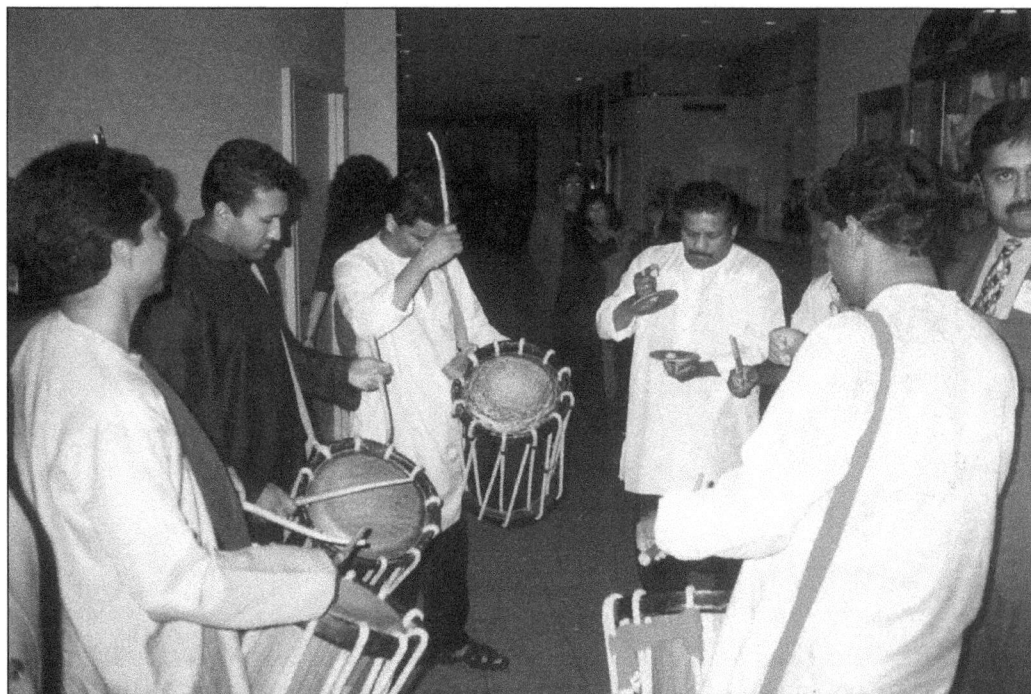

The *Chenda* Troupe, residents of Chicago with roots in the southern Indian state of Kerala, perform on traditional drums to usher in guests at the Indo-American Center's annual banquet at the Oak Brook Marriott in 1999. (Courtesy of Indo-American Center.)

Photographer Mukul Roy looks over the shoulder of Indo-American Center Board Member Sher Rajput as he examines her work on display at Schaumburg Township Public Library in the mid-1980s. Since the mid-1970s, Roy has diligently documented life in the Asian Indian community in Chicago with an artistic eye. (Courtesy of Prem Sharma.)

A mural display provides a backdrop for classical dancer Ahalya Satkunaratnam's performance at a 2001 Indo-American Center reception for *Changing Worlds*, an exhibition of immigrant photos and stories. The mural display depicting immigrant teenagers' changing worlds was created by students in a Taft High School art and writing project. (Photo by Kay Berkson.)

In March 1984, (left to right) Kiran Chaturvedi, Hoffman Estates Village President Virginia Mary Hayter, Dr. Sahu, and Dr. Raheja inaugurated the *Hindi Patshaala* (School) at the Highland Crossing Clubhouse. The school, founded by the Hindi Literary Society to preserve Hindi language and literature in the Chicago area, drew on teachers from the community to teach Hindi. (Photo by Mukul Roy.)

Following the Indian tradition of large poetry reading events, comic poets from India, Surendra Kumar (left) and Kaka Hathrasi (right), recite poetry at a 1989 *kavi sammelan* (poets' gathering) organized by the Hindi Literary Society to promote appreciation of Hindi language and literature. (Photo by Mukul Roy.)

Among numerous Asian Indian scholars at the University of Chicago, A.K. Ramanujan excelled not only as a professor, but also as a translator of poems and folk tales from Tamil and Kannada into English. In 1983, he received a MacArthur Foundation fellowship and, in 1986, was awarded the title of *Padma Shri* by the government of India for his contributions to Indian literature and linguistics. (Photo by Mukul Roy.)

Namasté America author Padma Rangaswamy chats with her Ph.D. thesis advisor, University of Illinois History Professor Leo Schelbert, and his wife, Virginia, during the launch of her book at the Chicago Historical Society in 2000. Based on her thesis research, *Namasté America: Indian Immigrants in An American Metropolis* is the first scholarly monograph on Chicago's Asian Indian population. (Courtesy of Indo-American Center.)

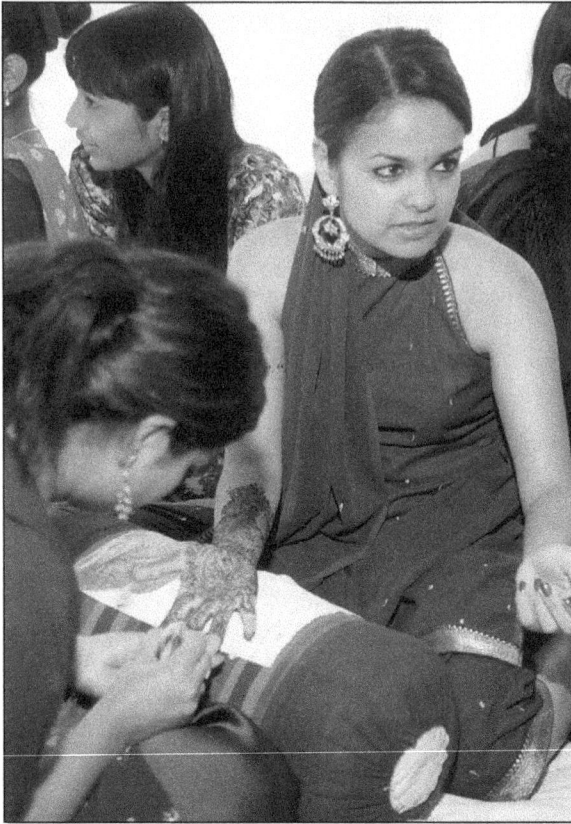

As part of bridal preparation, a *Mehendi* artist creates intricate designs made with henna on Chinar Shah's hands and feet before her marriage to Amit Sheth of Vernon Hills in 2001. *Mehendi* was embraced by Western pop culture when temporary tattoos became the vogue in the 1990s. (Courtesy of Panna Sheth.)

As the 20th century drew to a close, Chicago's cultural institutions began to recognize the importance of establishing links with the city's ethnic populations. The Field Museum's 2002 Cultural Connections program kick-off featured collaborative creation of a *rangoli*, a design for the protection and well being of the entire group. The project was supervised by Evanston artist Indira Freitas Johnson, founder and president of Shanti Foundation for Peace, established in 1993 to promote non-violence and to celebrate diversity through the arts. (Courtesy of Indira Freitas Johnson.)

Seven

ENTERTAINMENT
SPORT AND PASTIME

While Indian Americans enjoy socializing in each other's homes at every opportunity, team and individual recreational sports are also popular. A favorite activity for the various associations and large family gatherings is the picnic, at which children and adults engage in informal sports activities. Some associations like the Punjabi Cultural Society organize sports competitions in softball and volleyball and also Indian games such as "kabbadi." Second generation Indians have formed basketball teams which engage in friendly competition. Indians also enjoy golf and tennis, but they are most passionate about cricket, a game that England popularized during the colonial period in India.

Technological advances in satellite communication have spawned a thriving entertainment industry. Print and broadcast media have responded to the immigrants' thirst for information from their native country with a spate of ethnic newspapers in English and many of India's regional languages, while radio and TV channels offer the latest in entertainment from Bollywood (a commonly used term for Bombay's film industry.)

"Look, no hands!" Children compete in a cookie-eating contest at a Chicagoland forest preserve picnic organized by the Bengali Association of Greater Chicago in the 1970s. (Photo by Mukul Roy.)

Members of the Club of Indian Women (from left) Suman Katyal, Suman Mohlajee, Malti Sharma, and Promila Bansal gather in member Prem Sharma's home in 1988 to learn how to make *kachoris* (spicy stuffed pastry), a popular North Indian delicacy. (Photo by Mukul Roy.)

University students relax in a cafeteria after a fast food meal. Indian students have formed many different associations on campus based on their cultural, religious, and professional interests, and often hang out together, enjoying the camaraderie that comes from a shared ethnic background. (Courtesy of *India Tribune*.)

Indians play ping pong or table tennis, as it is more popularly known in India, at an Oak Brook community recreation center in 1985. It is common for basements in Indian homes to be equipped with tables for ping pong and billiards. (Photo by Mukul Roy.)

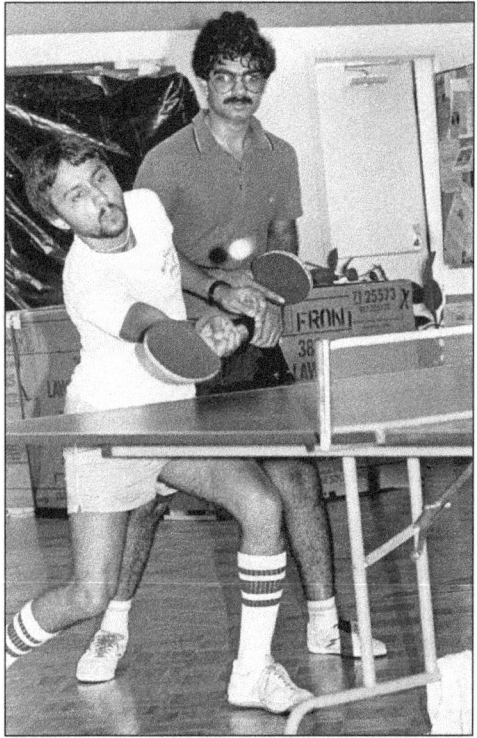

The Billimoria family relaxes over a game of carrom in the basement of their Kenilworth home in the early 1980s. This carrom board was brought from Mumbai as oversized luggage, but by the 1990s, shops on Devon Avenue began carrying them in response to demand from Indian families. (Photo by Mukul Roy.)

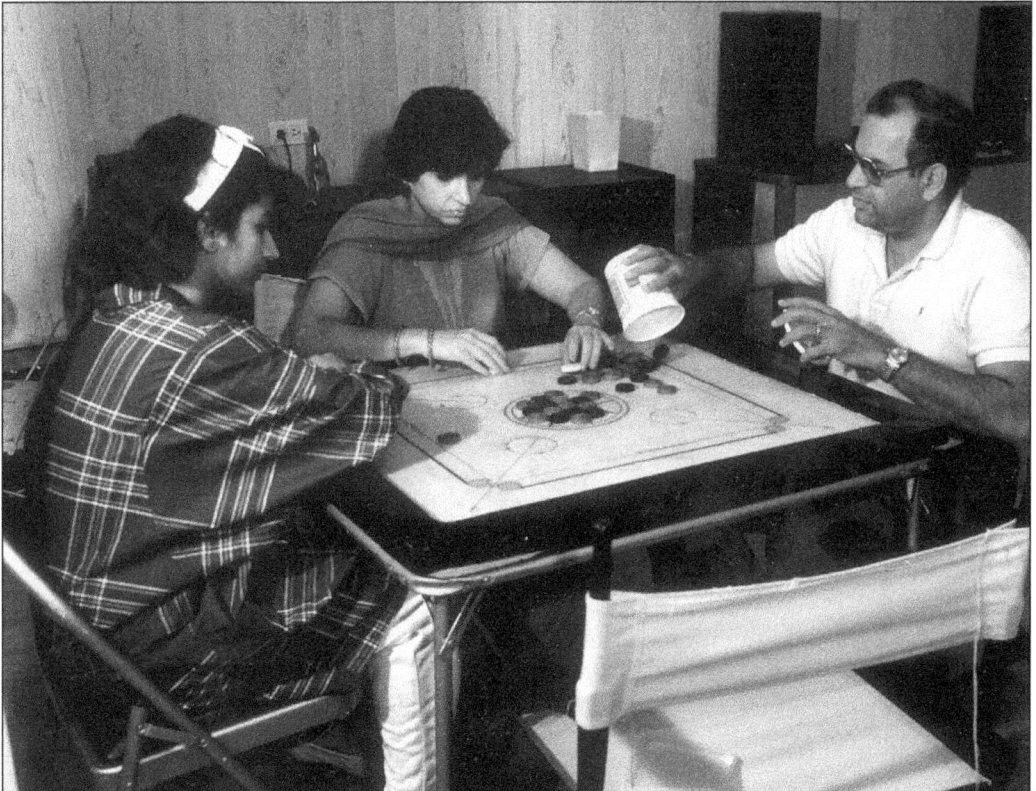

Volleyball is a game that Indians enjoy in an informal setting. Many regional associations organize volleyball tournaments at their sports gatherings. (Photo by Mukul Roy.)

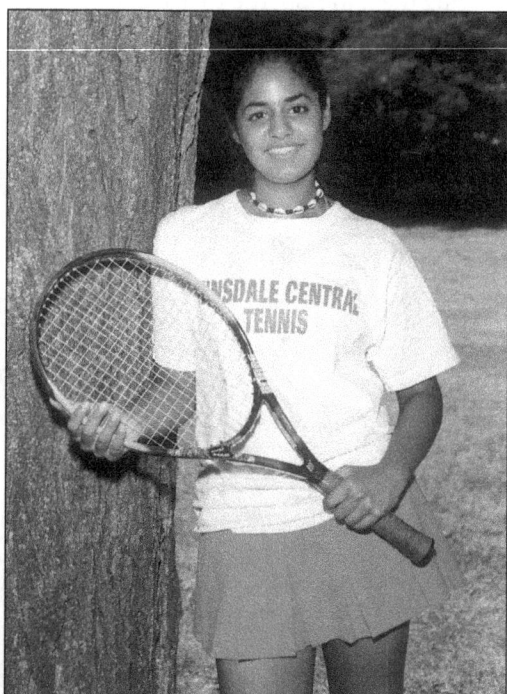

Sisters Madhuri (left) and Maithili Jha, from Hinsdale Central High, are nationally ranked tennis players and have won many tournaments. Maithili is currently captain of the University of Rochester tennis team while Madhuri, at age 15, is nationally ranked in the 16-year-old group. Tennis is a popular sport among both first and second generation Indians. (Courtesy of Vijay and Aruna Jha.)

Chicago area golfing enthusiasts, (from left) Subhash Agarwal, Nishendu Baxi, Ravi Sansguiri, Sughni Sukhani, and Shashi Kudchadker, relax during a game on their vacation in San Juan, Puerto Rico, in November 2002. Golf is a favorite sport among well-to-do Indians and is frequently a father-son activity. (Courtesy of Subhash Agarwal.)

The Punjabi *Kabbadi* team forms a circle in preparation for action. *Kabbadi* is a contact sport that calls for great agility and teamwork, and is a favorite with Punjabis who have transported it from the villages of their homeland to the parks of Chicago. (Courtesy of Punjabi Cultural Society.)

A visiting Indian professional cricket team poses with a team of Chicagoland cricketers following an exhibition match in June 1985 at a park in Chicago's south side. A unique sports culture of cricket leagues and tournaments has developed among people in Chicago from England and its former colonies: India, Pakistan, Bangladesh, Sri Lanka, the Caribbean, and Australia. (Photo by Mukul Roy.)

Cricketers in their whites dot the greens of Washington Park. Some suburban park districts have been persuaded to add the cricket "pitch" (a long runner strip on which the ball is bowled) to the baseball "diamond," so cricket lovers can enjoy the game in their adopted land. Satellite companies do brisk business when cricket fans sign up to watch international matches on "pay-per-view" TV. (Courtesy of Mridu and Chandra Sekhar.)

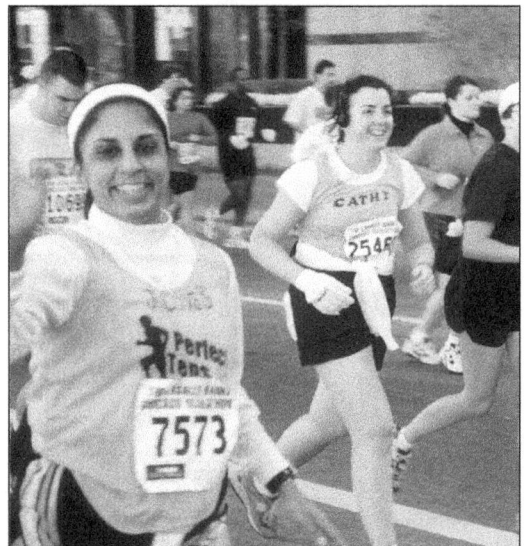

Prabha Parameswaran (left) waves to her family and friends as she runs the Chicago Marathon in October 1999. Like many other second-generation Indian Americans, Prabha, who is a Chicago area attorney, takes time from her busy professional life to participate in sporting events. (Courtesy of Prabha Parameswaran.)

Beauty pageants have grown from modest beginnings to glamorous mega events with international participation. Indian women dressed in western evening gowns compete for the crown at the first *India Tribune* Beauty Pageant at the Pick Congress Hotel in May 1982. From local contests, winners go on to the Miss India USA Pageant. Ms. Simi Ranajee, a native Chicagoan, was chosen as the first Miss India Worldwide in 1990. (Photo by Mukul Roy.)

Funkadesi was one of the earliest bands to integrate Indian music (Hindi film, folk, and classical) with reggae, funk, and Afro-Caribbean rhythms. A two-time Chicago Musical Award winner in the Contribution to World Music category, the band has received worldwide critical acclaim and gained a strong multicultural fan base. Band members include (from left, male) Valroy Dawkins, Abdul Hakim, Meshach Silas, Inder Paul Singh, Carlos Antonio Cornier, Maninder Singh, and Rahul Sharma; and (female) Kristin McGee and Radhika Chimata. (Courtesy of *Funkadesi*.)

Ariyan International

Proudly Presents

DESPLAINES THEATER   ADELPHI THEATER
Tel: 847.803.6741, Tel: 847.323.1072   Tel: 773-262-3456, Tel: 773-262-FILM

RELEASING ON SEPT. 8TH 2000

JAYA BACHCHAN   KARINA KAPOOR   HRITHIK ROSHAN

For more Info & Schedule
Visit our Web Site
WWW.HINDICINEMA.COM
E-MAIL
DESPLAINESTHEATER@HOTMAIL.COM

Witness
The most amazing
9 min Tanday Dance
Performed by
HRITHIK

fiza फ़िज़ा

Bollywood blockbusters are released simultaneously on Indian and American screens and play to packed houses. Neighborhood theaters such as Adelphi on Clark Street were losing money to the multiplexes when Indian businesses bought them up and started screening Bollywood hits such as this one featuring Indian heartthrob Hrithik Roshan.

Members of the Indian community gather outside Chicago Theater on State Street for a live show featuring Indian movie stars in the 1980s. As the shows got bigger and more elaborate, they had to be staged in much larger spaces such as the Rosemont Horizon or the UIC Pavilion. (Courtesy of Prem Sharma.)

Chitrahar, a locally produced TV show, offers variety programming that includes music and dance from Indian TV as well as local talent. (From left) Mohammed Ali, Umesh Sharma, Vichitra Nayyar, daughters Anjali and Alka, and Tara Swaminathan perform at an annual *Chitrahar* night. Vichitra, who founded *Chitrahar* in 1982, has handed over the reins to her daughter Anjali. The program has survived competition from internationally syndicated shows which are offered on numerous satellite channels. Radio stations also air programs in various regional languages. (Courtesy of Prem Sharma.)

Chicago's first Indian cable TV program *Bharat Darshan* is run by Super Broadcasting Company or SBC. Their float at the 1996 Indian Independence Day parade on Devon Avenue advertises their community presence. (Courtesy of *India Tribune.*)

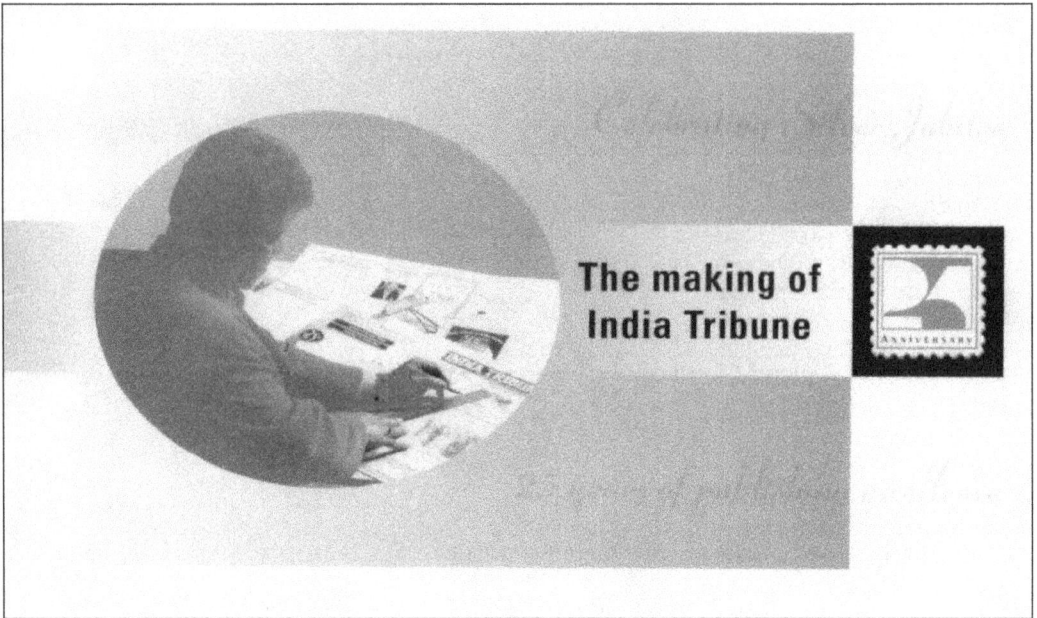

India Tribune, the longest-running Chicago-based Indian newspaper focusing mainly on local news of the immigrant community, was started in 1977. This souvenir was published on the occasion of its 25th anniversary in 2002. (Courtesy of *India Tribune*.)

Journalists from Chicago's Indian newspapers, (left to right) Moin Khan of *Spotlight*, Thakur Bhai Patel of *India West*, Nand Kapoor of *News India*, Ramesh Soparawala of *India Abroad*, and Prashant Shah of *India Tribune*, share a rare moment together in the 1980s. Although some newspapers have changed management and others have gone under, ethnic Indian print media in Chicago continues to thrive with the advent of later weeklies such as *Indian Reporter* and *India West*. There are several publications in regional languages such as Gujarati, Malayalam, Punjabi, and Urdu. (Photo by Mukul Roy.)

Eight

POLITICS

GETTING INVOLVED

There are various ways in which Chicago's Indian Americans get involved in the political process, both at the national and local levels. Indians have acquired American citizenship through naturalization in record numbers, enjoying its benefits and laying the foundation for political involvement. Since India allowed dual citizenship in 2003, Indian Americans have greater opportunity to participate more actively in the development of their country of origin.

Chicago is a Democratic stronghold, so it is not surprising that the leading Indian political body in the city is the Indo-American Democratic Organization. Established in 1980, it has grown in influence by endorsing political candidates who seek the support of the Indian community, conducting voter registration drives, sending delegates to national political conventions, and teaming up with other ethnic groups to lobby on issues such as affirmative action, immigration, and discrimination. It has also actively encouraged members of the U.S. Congress to join the Congressional Caucus on India and Indian Americans, which voices Indian American concerns in Washington D.C. In the suburbs, where affluent Indians tend to be more widely scattered than they are in the city, voting patterns tend to be bi-partisan.

Despite efforts to consolidate voters in the redistricting process, Indian Americans are splintered into different districts. They have generally used their political clout to support non-Indians who are sensitive to their needs and sympathetic to India in international relations. However, in Niles Township, their concentration in the northwest suburbs has helped them elect Indian Americans to local office.

Democratic National Committee member Ann Lata Kalayil (extreme left), the first woman president of the Indo-American Democratic Organization (IADO), and IADO members Selma D'Souza and Rupal Dalal (right) attend a White House reception hosted by President Bill Clinton in March 1999. (Courtesy of Ann Lata Kalayil.)

At a reception hosted by Bell Telephone Company following the Naturalization Ceremony on July 26, 1966 at the Dirksen Federal Building in Chicago, Surendra P. Shah (center), accompanied by his wife, Dorothie, was invited to say a few remarks on behalf of the 33 new citizens. He explained, "Almost unlimited opportunities to pursue happiness, both material and spiritual, and the warm, unreserved acceptance of Americans motivated my decision to become a U.S. citizen." American laws and attitudes had changed greatly from an earlier era. From 1922 through 1931 the Cable Act decreed that female (but not male) citizens who married aliens ineligible for citizenship would lose their own citizenship. J. Edgar Hoover himself dubbed the Cable Act "the damnedest law he ever saw." (Courtesy of Dorothie Shah.)

Jody Wadhwa, retired business executive and trustee of Oakton Community College, ran for State Representative in the 57th district. Though his bid for office in the 2000 election was unsuccessful, it demonstrated the ability and willingness of Indian Americans to participate in the political process. The only Indian American ever elected to nation-wide public office was Congressman Dalip Singh Saund, from California (first elected in 1958 and reelected twice subsequently). (Courtesy of Jody Wadhwa.)

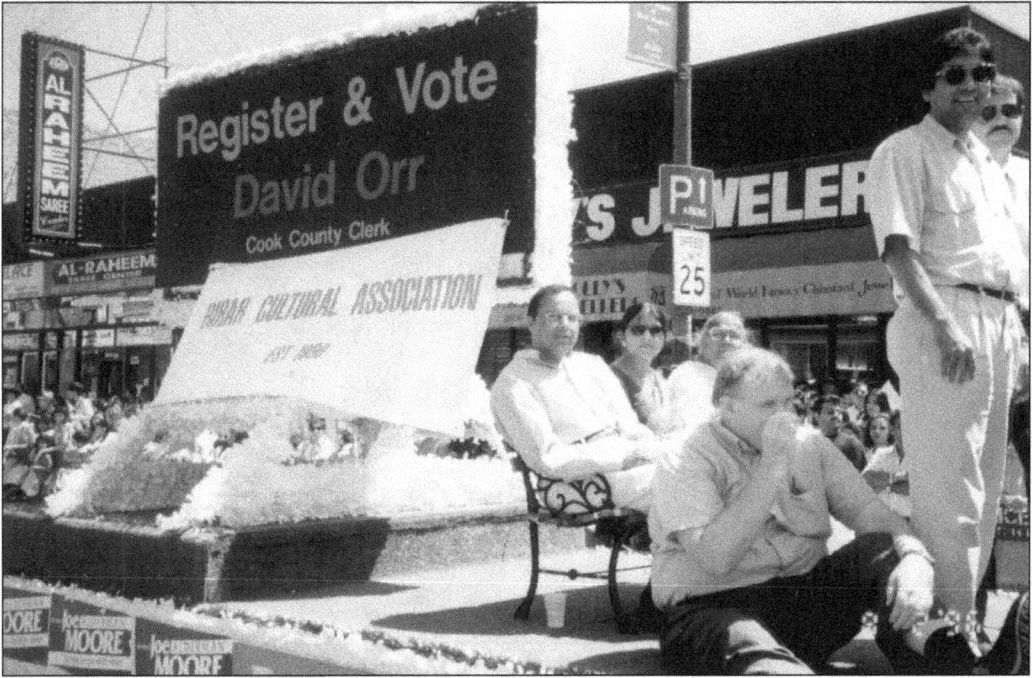

The 1996 Indian Independence Day parade float on Devon Avenue sponsored by the Bihar Cultural Association urges Indians to register and vote for Democrats David Orr (Cook County Clerk) and Joe Moore (49th Ward Alderman). (Courtesy of *India Tribune*.)

Two Indian Americans were elected to public office in 2000 from Niles Township—Collector Pramod Shah (standing extreme left) and Trustee Usha Kamaria (seated, second from right). They are pictured here with their colleagues on the Niles Township Board. (Courtesy of Pramod Shah.)

Indian Americans show their support for Democratic Mayoral candidate Michael Bilandic at a 1977 rally organized by Asian Americans for Bilandic at the Drake Hotel. Philip Kalayil (extreme left) is one of the co-founders of the Indo-American Democratic Organization (IADO). The lady in the sari is his wife, Annamma Kalayil. (Courtesy of Ann Lata Kalayil.)

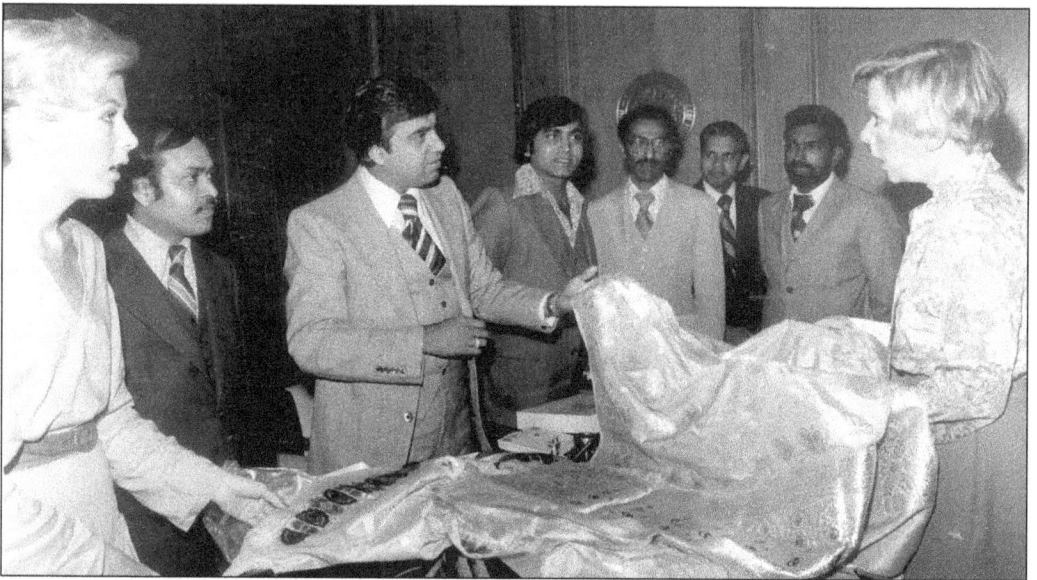

Members of the Indian community visit Mayor Jane Byrne in city hall and suggest that she wear a sari to IADO's first banquet in 1980. Pictured from left to right are Kathy Byrne (the mayor's daughter), Ranjit Ganguly (President, IADO), Ratan Sharma (India Sari Palace), Amrit Patel (Patel Brothers), Philip Kalayil (Secretary, IADO), Babubhai Contractor (Treasurer, IADO), Mathew Kurien (Kavita Imports) and Chicago Mayor Jane Byrne. (Courtesy of Ranjit Ganguly.)

In keeping with their tradition of support for Democratic mayoral candidates, officers of the Indo-American Democratic Organization line up alongside Harold Washington at an awards ceremony. Pictured from left to right are Bapu Arekapudi, Roy Thomas, Philip Kalayil, Ranjit Ganguly, Harold Washington, and Tirupatiah Tella. (Courtesy of Ann Lata Kalayil.)

State's Attorney Richard M. Daley meets with Indian Americans at a 1988 banquet. The community's support for Daley pre-dates his election as Mayor of Chicago. (Courtesy of Ann Lata Kalayil.)

Jim Edgar, Illinois Governor (1991–99), appointed Rajinder Mago (extreme left) and Prem Sharma (center), representatives of the Indian American community, to the Governor's Advisory Council on Asian American Affairs. (Courtesy of Prem Sharma.)

Republican Illinois State Comptroller Loleta Didrickson, guest of honor at the 1995 Club of Indian Women annual dinner dance, is joined by club members Shashi Kathpalia (left) and Asha Singhal. Though the Club of Indian Women is an apolitical organization, it has feted women politicians in recognition of their achievements. (Courtesy of *India Tribune*.)

Senator Paul Simon (D-IL, 1984–1997) was considered a friend of India, and, thanks to the efforts of Chicago area physicians, introduced legislation to ban discrimination against foreign medical graduates. Here he is seen with Virendra Bisla (left), young Sudeep Bisla, and Amrish Mahajan (right). (Photo by Urmilla Chawla.)

Among more than 200 members of the Indian American medical community who met with Senator Edward Kennedy (D-MA) in Bukhara restaurant were (left to right) Drs. Kumud Burman, Ashutosh Gupta, Pratap Kumar, Shastri Swaminathan, Senator Kennedy, Viren Desai, Vijay Kulkarni, and Virendra Bisla. The Senator promised to back Simon's bill and retain the 5th preference category for relatives of U.S. immigrants in the revision of immigration law. Politicians wooing Indian American votes and their contributions consider Chicago an important stop on the campaign trail. (Photo by Urmilla Chawla.)

When Carol Moseley-Braun (D-IL, U.S. Senate, 1994–1998) became the first African American woman to be elected to the U.S. Senate, she did so with help from the Indian American community. Here she is seen at a fundraiser with (standing, from left) Vijayalakshmi Arekapudi, Ann Lata Kalayil, Ashref Hashim, Ashutosh Gupta, and Niranjan Shah. Seated with her is State Senator Howard Carroll. (Courtesy of Ann Lata Kalayil.)

Indian Independence Day parades are organized by the Federation of India Associations (FIA), which regularly invites elected officials to lead the march. The 2000 Devon Avenue parade featured (left to right) Iftekar Shareef (President, FIA), Terry O'Brien (President, Water Reclamation District), Congresswoman Janice Schakowsky (D-IL, 9th district which includes the Devon Avenue neighborhood), Congressman Rod Blagojevich (D-IL, 5th district), Richard Devine (State's Attorney), Surendra Kumar (Consul General of India, Chicago) and Niranjan Shah (FIA Trustee). (Courtesy of *India Tribune*.)

Left: Hillary Clinton, Democratic Senator from New York, campaigned at a Michigan Avenue hotel in 2000 at a fundraiser organized by Niranjan Shah, who is cofounder and CEO of Globetrotters Engineering Corporation that has worked on major city projects at O'Hare International Airport and the Deep Tunnel Project. (Courtesy of *India Tribune*.)

Right: Democratic National Committee delegate Smita Shah appears with Hollywood celebrity Kevin Costner at the national convention in Los Angeles in 2000. Smita was the youngest-ever Indian American delegate to the convention in 1996. She served as an intern in the office of Leon Panetta, White House Chief of Staff. (Courtesy of Niranjan Shah.)

Democratic delegates from Illinois to the Los Angeles convention in 2000 included (from left) Rod Blagojevich (Illinois congressman elected Governor in 2002), Rena M. Van Tine (the first Indian American judge in Illinois), Super Delegate Ann Lata Kalayil, Selma D'Souza (vice-president, IADO) and Lisa Madigan (Illinois state senator elected attorney general in 2002). (Courtesy of Ann Lata Kalayil.)

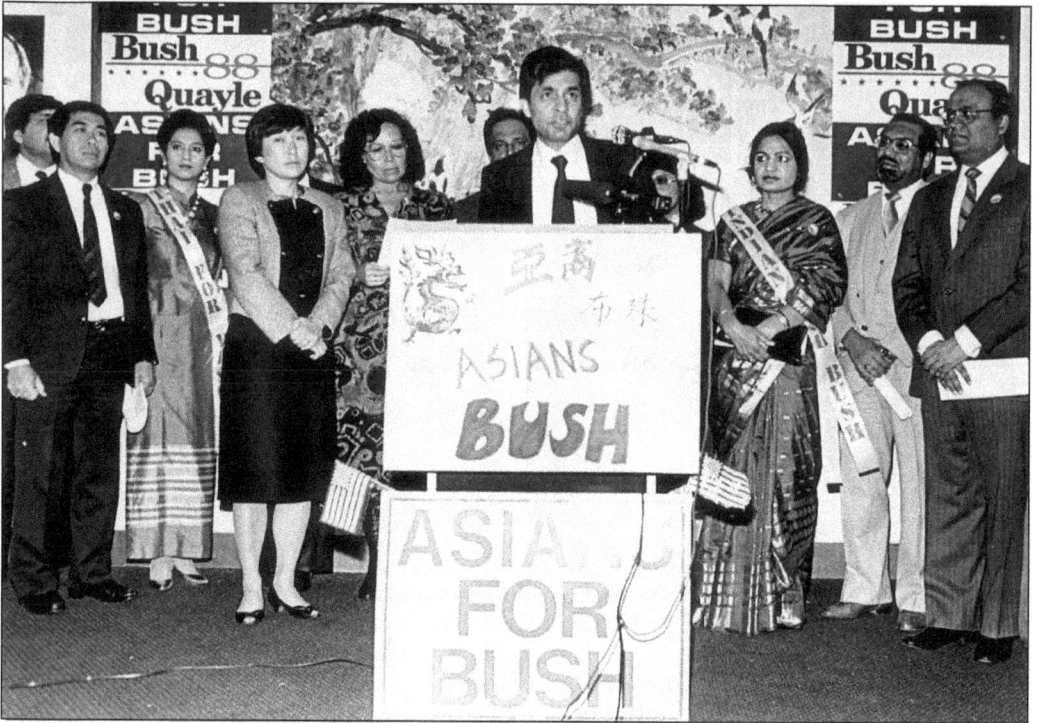

Though Indian Americans, especially in the city, are heavily Democratic, there are also many Republicans among them in the suburbs. Here Indian Americans join other Asians to show their support for the Bush-Quayle ticket in 1988. (Photo by Mukul Roy.)

In 1995, the American Association of Physicians of Indian Origin (AAPI) raised over a million dollars for President Bill Clinton, the featured speaker at their 13th annual conference held in Chicago. Seated are Prem Rupani, President of the India Medical Association of Illinois (left) and Gopal Lalmalani, President of AAPI. This was the first time that a sitting president addressed an Indian association. The event was marked with great fanfare in the Indian community. (Photo by Mukul Roy.)

100

Nine

SERVICE
FULFILLING NEEDS

Many Asian Indians who have prospered in the United States share their good fortune with others by volunteering and contributing generously to worthy causes. In addition to established mainstream institutions, which provide abundant avenues for service, a plethora of organizations addressing special needs and interests of immigrants has emerged as the population has grown. These organizations facilitate immigrant adjustment to America and American understanding of the distinctive heritage and customs of Asian Indians.

Despite the success of the majority of immigrants in adapting to a new homeland, strains of adjusting and coping with new challenges are evident in the immigrant community. Many elderly parents who have followed their children from India to the United States to care for grandchildren or simply to make new lives find the environment alien and unfriendly as do many young wives who have left behind large combined families. Those who arrive lacking professional degrees or fluency in English face limited employment opportunities. Among problems faced by some immigrants are social isolation, domestic abuse, lack of access to health care, and reluctance to seek help outside the traditional extended family.

Many Asian Indian immigrants concerned about problems in India such as lack of education and employment opportunities, exploitation of women and children, inadequate sanitation and healthcare, and environmental issues are working to address problems there. Donations of talent, time, and money benefit those in need and provide gratification for the donors.

Indo-American Center (IAC) volunteers Lakshmi Menon, Indira Adusumilli, and Sushila Maker greet a visitor at the 1997 press conference inaugurating the City of Chicago Ethnic Neighborhood Tours. IAC volunteers offer tour participants an informative introduction to the immigrant community and a Devon Avenue walking tour of "India in Chicago." Visitors learn about distinctive customs while they converse with Asian Indians and examine specialty items offered in neighborhood shops. (Courtesy of Chicago Neighborhood Tours, Chicago Office of Tourism.)

The importance Asian Indians place on education prompts families to take an active interest in their children's schooling and to participate in parent-teacher organizations. PTA volunteer Gauri Padhiar and students meet with Chicago Public School teacher Naseem Umar (center) at Volta School in 2000. (Courtesy of Naseem Umar.)

Godrej Billimoria (right), accompanied by his wife, Avan, received the 2001 Rotarian of the Year award presented by Dr. Frank Develin, President of Rotary International. Billimoria, a member of the International Committee of the Wilmette Rotary Club since 1982, was recognized for his volunteer achievements, which led to Rotary sponsorship of almost $100,000 worth of projects including equipment for a hospital for the blind in India. (Courtesy of Avan Billimoria.)

102

Members of the India Development Service (IDS) Board of Directors and volunteers assemble after an educational seminar in 1992. IDS was established in 1974 by a group of Asian Indians in Chicago as a vehicle to aid disadvantaged people in their land of origin. Managed entirely by volunteers, IDS funds small economic and social development projects in India "to empower the disadvantaged to become self reliant." In order to increase awareness, IDS regularly schedules screenings of socially conscious films and presentations by speakers such as economist Amartya Sen, 1998 Nobel prize winner. (Courtesy of IDS.)

NATIONAL CONFERENCE FOR SUSTAINABLE DEVELOPMENT IN INDIA
ILLINOIS INSTITUTE OF TECHNOLOGY

Dr. Geeta Maker-Clark joined her hostess Kaure and Kaure's children in their Rajasthani village in 1997 when she led a tour of American medical students who were learning about the benefits of folk medicine from village practitioners. After graduation from Northwestern University, Geeta established a mobile medical clinic with an IDS supported non-governmental organization in Andhra Pradesh. In an effort to engage youth in their projects, IDS organizes externship opportunities connecting second generation Asian Indians with grass roots projects in India. (Courtesy of Geeta Maker-Clark.)

The Meena Bazaar, an annual ethnic fair, sponsored by the Club of Indian Women (CIW), is one of their fundraising events, which enables them to contribute support to Apna Ghar, Asian Human Services, and IDS. CIW, which began as a social group in 1978, was the first Asian American women's group in the Chicago area. In 1993, CIW established a social group for senior citizens. The club has provided unique opportunities for women to develop leadership and organizational skills. (Courtesy of Prem Sharma.)

CIW members Suman Katyal (left) and Bhadra Bhuva packed donated clothing for distribution to the needy. Recognizing the urgency to respond to women in distress, in 1983, CIW opened the Indo-Crisis Line to assist women facing severe problems of adjustment to a new environment. This proved especially valuable for women with limited English language skills and provided the groundwork for a shelter for battered South Asian women and their children. (Courtesy of Prem Sharma.)

104

With the absence of traditional sources of support, instances of domestic violence in the immigrant community became an urgent matter, and in 1989, Apna Ghar, the first shelter for South Asian women in the United States, was established in Chicago. Staff members (left to right facing the table): Manju Vats; Heather Stahl; and K. Sujata, executive director, (1999–) are shown participating in a 2002 art therapy project, "Cocoon/Butterfly." Arts activities are utilized to enhance the sense of dignity and self-respect of victims of abuse at Apna Ghar where services seek to break the cycle of violence. (Courtesy of Apna Ghar.)

Kanta Khipple, (standing third from left) a founder of Apna Ghar, was among outstanding Chicagoans recognized in 1991 with rocks inscribed in their honor and scattered throughout the Chicago loop. Accompanying her are Prem Sharma, (second from left) Apna Ghar Board president, and Abha Pandya, (right), who later became executive director of Asian Human Services. Lee Maglaya and Anil Pandya kneel in front by the rock. (Courtesy of Apna Ghar.)

G.S. Punia, the Indo-American Center's immigration coordinator, demonstrates a turban wrap during an Ethnic Dialogue session with a school group at the Center. The sessions are part of IAC's Education Project that promotes understanding of and respect for Asian Indian heritage and culture through outreach projects and teacher workshops. The quilt, featuring symbols of religions of India in the background, was created by fifth graders at Bell School and their teacher Jane Grant, an IAC teacher program participant. (Courtesy of Indo-American Center.)

Students at an elementary school in India enjoy an art lesson taught by Robert Langston, Morgan Park Academy art teacher, during a Fulbright-funded study-tour of India organized by the Indo-American Center in 1997. An Indian American study-tour colleague, Manjula Singh, Morton West High School history teacher, served as interpreter. Langston subsequently hosted a Fulbright grant visit to Chicago of New Delhi artist, Prasanta Mukherjee, who conducted workshops for the Indo-American Center's Summer Fun program for neighborhood children. (Photo by Patricia Riddiford.)

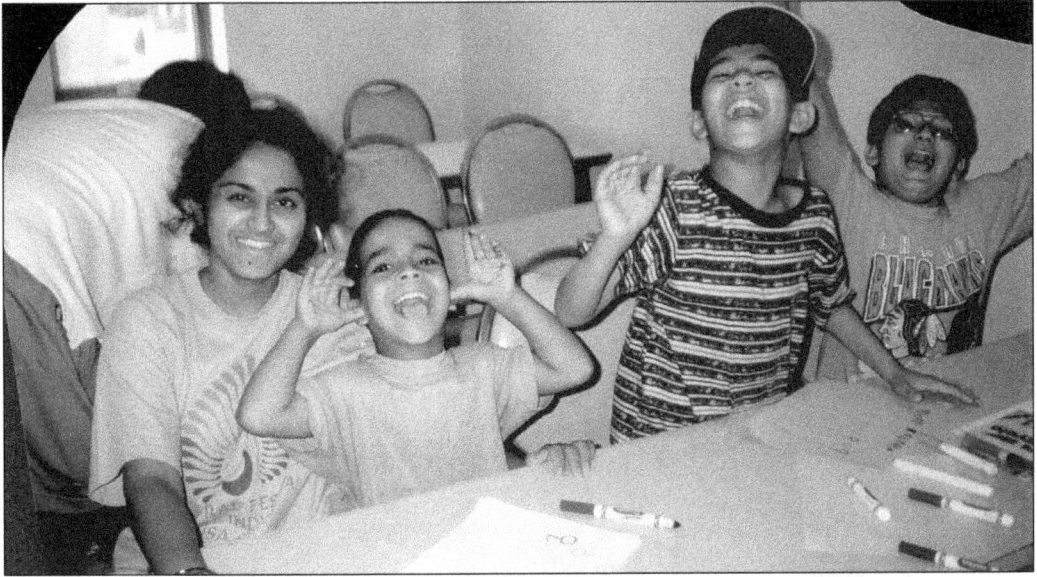

NetIP member Minoti Amin (left) Volunteer Youth Tutoring Coordinator at the Indo-American Center in 1998, takes a break with neighborhood youngsters during a Summer Fun session. The Network of Young Indian Professionals (NetIP) founded in Chicago in 1990 is primarily a social organization, but from its outset it also fostered community service, and many members have volunteered at IAC, offering computer instruction, English tutoring, and fund-raising assistance. (Courtesy of Indo-American Center.)

The Association for the Advancement of Indian Immigrants in America (AAIIA) assists immigrants in adjusting to a new environment. Enjoying an AAIIA youth mentoring program outing are (left to right) Dolly Shah, Jitesh Thakkar, Nina Gandhi, Kartik Patel, Vikas Upadhyay, Amar Patel, Aiyush Joshi, Shilpa Amin, Vipin Jain, Saloni Shah, Sneha Kothari, Ami Patel, and Munu Gandhi. AAIIA also awards scholarships for community service and academic achievement. (Courtesy of AAIIA.)

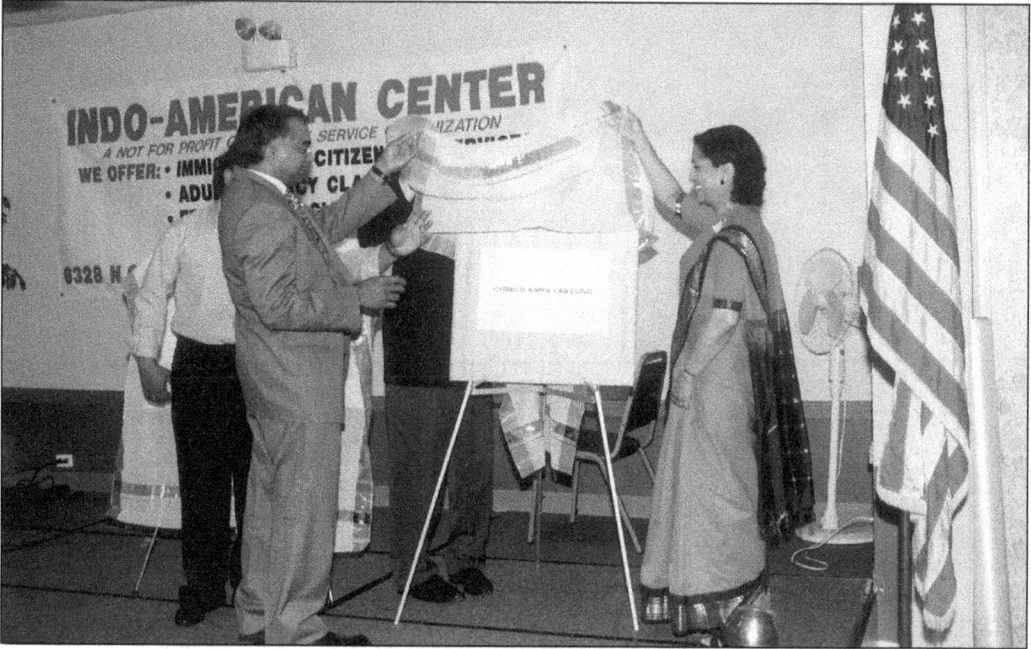

Indo-American Center Board member Bapu Arekapudi assists Valsa Kappil at the 1997 official inauguration of the legal clinic at the IAC. Established in memory of her husband, attorney Cyriac Kappil, to honor his commitment to the needy, the clinic offers low-income individuals the professional expertise of volunteer lawyers and conducts educational seminars. (Courtesy of Indo-American Center.)

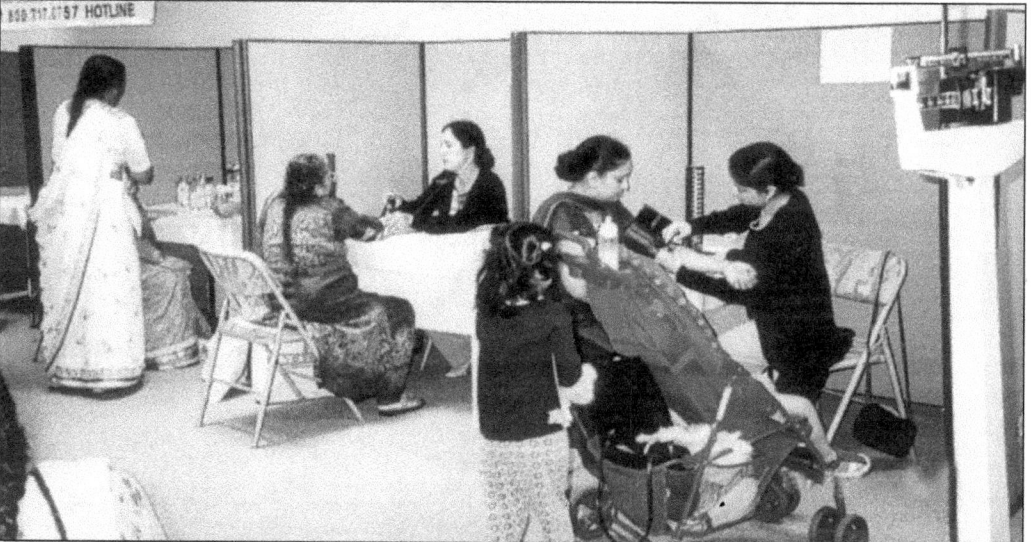

Many women and children attended a health fair conducted by the Indian American Medical Association (Illinois) Charitable Foundation (IAMACF) in September 2002. IAMACF provides basic and preventative health care for adults and children, free laboratory services and pharmacy, as well as public health education at their Sridhar Nimmagadda Memorial Clinic at 2645 W. Peterson. From 1994 until June 2002, the medical clinic was conducted at the Indo-American Center. (Courtesy of IAMACF.)

Volunteer Mrs. Dhanu Dhruv explains Social Security benefits to a group of immigrants gathered at Asian Human Services (AHS), which was established in 1978 to provide quality and compassionate services to the Asian American community of metropolitan Chicago. Staff members and dedicated volunteers respond to needs of an increasing population of Asian immigrants who speak a wide variety of languages. (Courtesy of Asian Human Services.)

Literacy students prepare for the U.S. citizenship test aided by volunteers who teach English and Civics classes at the Indo-American Center. IAC conducts regular educational and social activities for seniors and counsels eligible immigrants about assistance through the Public Benefits Outreach and Interpretation Project. (Courtesy of Indo-American Center.)

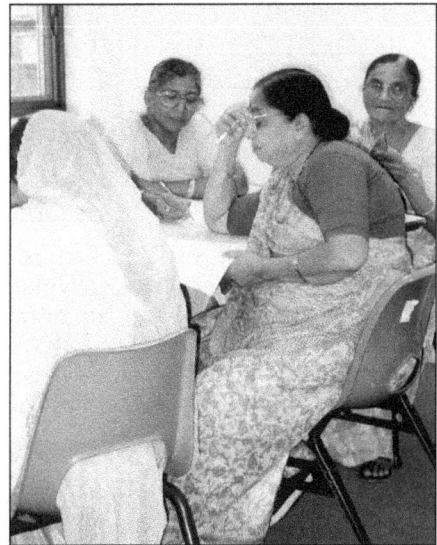

R.S. Rajan, executive director of the Indo-American Center, received an award from the City of Chicago Department of Human Services on May 27, 2000, in recognition of his services to the Asian senior community. The award was presented at the Asian American Seniors' Day event held at Warren Park. Center stage (left to right) are Cook County Attorney General Richard Devine; Kamalavalli, mother-in-law of award recipient; R.S. Rajan; and Ray Vasquez, commissioner, Department of Human Services. (Photo by S. Krishnan.)

To accommodate special needs of Asian and Middle Eastern immigrants in suburban communities, the Hamdard Center was established in 1993 in Wood Dale, Illinois. Multilingual professional staff members and volunteers provide counseling and legal assistance to individuals. The Center also operates a licensed shelter facility for victims of abuse. (Courtesy of the Hamdard Center.)

CARE and SHARE was launched in 1990 by a handful of professionals who felt compelled to reach out to less fortunate individuals by raising funds and recruiting volunteers to support established local charitable organizations and humanitarian efforts in India. CARE and SHARE helps the homeless through the Olive Branch Mission, those battling drug and alcohol addiction through Living Light Outreach Center, and victims of abuse through Apna Ghar and other shelters. (Courtesy of CARE and SHARE.)

Volunteers, Board members, and staff of the Indo-American Center join co-founders M.K.G. Pillay (1924–1994) (middle row, center) and Pratap Bhavnani (1914–1998) (third row, left) in 1993. (Courtesy of Indo-American Center.)

Ten

HOMELAND

STRENGTHENING LINKS

Indians who came to the United States did so seeking education and experience, not fleeing oppression, war, or famine. Moving from one secular, pluralistic democracy to another, they felt no desire to burn their bridges behind them, and instead, have maintained active and productive links to their land of origin. India is the only country with a specific designation for its expatriate population, "Non-resident Indians" or "NRIs"—a term that reminds expatriates of their heritage and makes them feel a part of the homeland, no matter how far away or how many generations removed they may be.

The prosperity of the immigrants, as well as the increasing ease of communication and travel, make it possible for family members in both countries to visit each other often. Many students return to India to marry, as do several members of the second generation. The movement between the two countries helps strengthen connections and renew traditions that might otherwise fade away.

Connections to the homeland expanded beyond the social and cultural spheres with the dawning of the global economy. Indians in business and industry established ventures that capitalized on the resources of their homeland. The immigrant community began to play a significant role in strengthening ties between India and the United States in both commercial and political arenas. Dignitaries from India frequently visited Chicago and other cities in the U.S. to strengthen links with expatriate members of their communities and to promote investment in their native regions. Many immigrants, eager to "give back," have involved themselves actively in humanitarian efforts in the country that nurtured and educated them in their youth.

Onlookers waving Indian flags cheer on the August 2000 India Independence Day parade along Devon Avenue. The annual parade is a joyous reaffirmation of the immigrants' connection to their land of origin and a celebration of their identity as ethnic Chicagoans. (Courtesy of *India Tribune*.)

Elderly parents who come to Chicago to live with their Indian immigrant children feel connected to the homeland through special community and religious events such as the JAINA convention, held at the Rosemont Convention Center from July 5 to July 8, 2001. Approximately 7,000 members of the Jain faith in North America attended the event. (Courtesy of *India Tribune*.)

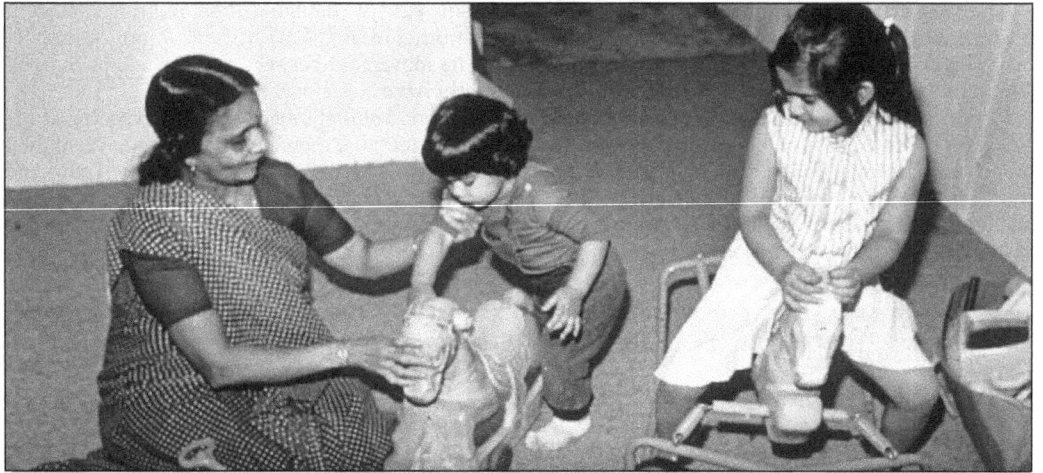

As retired parents of Indian immigrants started joining their children in Chicago in the late 1980s, they took over household and childcare tasks in the traditional Indian manner, thus reinforcing the next generation's awareness and sense of connection with the land of origin. (Photo by Mukul Roy.)

Meera Sanghani in Kapotasana

• Yoga classes
• Yoga workshops
• Yoga wear

One East Oak Street • Suite 3W • Chicago, IL 6061
312-587-7492 • www.priyayoga.com
& boutique

Meera V. Sanghani, a teacher at the Priya Yoga Studio and volunteer yoga instructor at the Indo-American Center says, "There's definitely a strong element of pride in the fact that yoga originated in my country. I am an Indian-American woman. I struggled for many years trying to find a connection to my culture that I feel comfortable with. I finally found one." (Courtesy of Meera Sanghani.)

112

Indian religious groups in the United States maintain strong links with the spiritual leadership of the homeland. On September 3, 1973, Archbishop Simon Lourdusamy of Bangalore, India, was presented with a Mahatma Gandhi medallion at a reception sponsored by the India Christian Association. With the Archbishop are (from right) Cyriac Poovathunkal, vice president; Theodore G. Mazarello, president; Eustace Pereira, vice consul of India; and Phillip T. Kalayil, public relations chairman. (Courtesy Ann Lata Kalayil.)

India's beloved singer Lata Mangeshkar (right) stands with her sister at the 1985 opening ceremony of the Hindu Temple of Greater Chicago. Built in Lemont in the traditional style of ancient temples in India, it is the first house of worship constructed for Hindus in the Chicago area. (Photo by Mukul Roy.)

Sitar maestro Pandit Ravi Shankar poses with Prem Sharma at a concert sponsored by the Ameer Khusro Society in 1984. Shankar pioneered bridging the gap between music of the East and West and has collaborated with Western artists and composers including Sir Yehudi Menuhin and Philip Glass. The Ameer Khusro Society, founded to foster interest in Indian classical music and poetry, held its first event in 1982—a week-long Tansen festival featuring 24-hour days of performances from the renowned Moghul court musician's works. (Courtesy of Prem Sharma.)

Renowned Indian dancer and actress Vyjayantimala (front row, third from left) shares a light moment with Hema Rajagopalan (left), founder of *Natyakalalayam*; daughter, Krithika Rajagopalan (foreground); Indian scholar and Columbia College professor Joan Erdman; and friends at a reception in the Rajagopalans' Oak Brook home in 1994. (Photo by Mukul Roy.)

Members of the Club of Indian Women surround Indian actress and activist Shabana Azmi at a luncheon hosted by Club president Urmilla Chawla at her home. Standing from left: Manju Gupta, Urmilla Chawla, Prem Sehgal, Shabana Azmi, Suman Mohlajee, Suman Katyal, Rashmi Jain, and (seated) Bhadra Bhuva. Shabana is a frequent visitor to Chicago where she performs in theatrical productions and speaks at fundraisers for social causes in the Indian immigrant community. (Courtesy of *India Tribune*.)

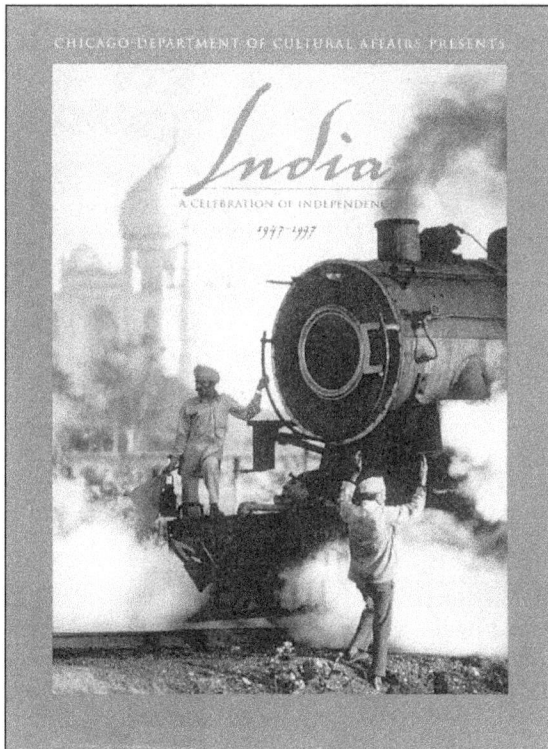

In 1999, the Chicago Cultural Center hosted "India: A Celebration of Independence 1947–1997," an exhibition featuring images of the human face and inner life of India by internationally renowned photographers. In conjunction with the exhibition, the Indo-American Center collaborated with the Chicago Department of Cultural Affairs to conduct a teachers' workshop: "Focus on India: An Exploration Through the Camera Lens." A Humanities Festival Indian Puppet Theater performance by Bhartiya Lok Kala Mandal from Rajasthan was included in the workshop program. (Courtesy of the City of Chicago Department of Cultural Affairs.)

115

An August 2000 Raj Kapoor retrospective marked the beginning of a series of special screenings of Indian films organized at the Gene Siskel Film Center by Surendra Kumar, Consul General of India. The films further enhanced widening appreciation of Indian cinema. "They are a very important tool of cultural diplomacy," according to Kumar. "I know these films are bringing the world closer." (Courtesy of the Consulate General of India.)

The *Apna Sangeet* group from England is honored by the Punjabi Cultural Society of Chicago following its performance at the Punjabi Cultural Society Night on November 7, 1998, at India House Banquet in Schaumburg. Special events organized by various regional and spiritual groups attract members from India and from the Indian global diaspora to Chicago. (Courtesy of *India Tribune*.)

Professor Bala Balachandran (standing) addresses the 1994 annual seminar on business in India at Northwestern University's Kellogg School of Management, as U.K.-based Indian industrialist Swaraj Paul (second from left) listens. India's friendlier business climate has attracted many multi-national corporations seeking access to its growing markets. Professor Balachandran, who helped found the Information Resource Management Program at Northwestern in 1974, has earned numerous honors including the Padma Shri, one of India's highest awards, conferred on individuals who have distinguished themselves in their fields. (Photo by Mukul Roy.)

Telecommunications expert Satyen Pitroda, chairman and CEO of WorldTel, came to Chicago as a student following his graduation from engineering school in India. He served as Minister for National Technology Missions under Indian Prime Minister Rajiv Gandhi and revolutionized telecommunications in India by establishing small rural exchanges that made telephone service available to even remote and isolated villages. (Courtesy of India Development Service.)

The community's response to events in the homeland takes many shapes. On November 3, 1984, stunned Indian Americans joined a procession on Devon Avenue to mourn the assassination of Indian Prime Minister Indira Gandhi, the first woman ever elected to lead a democracy. (Photo by Mukul Roy.)

Following the assassination of former Prime Minister Rajiv Gandhi in May 1991, Illinois Governor Jim Edgar signs the condolence book at the Indian consulate as Consul-General of India Mr. P.L. Santoshi looks on. (Photo by Mukul Roy.)

The immigrant community maintains a pro-active approach in guarding against local outbreaks of hostility in response to events in their land of origin. Disturbed by the rise of religious animosity in their secular homeland, Indian immigrants organized a unity march on Devon Avenue in the wake of the December 1992 destruction of the Babri Masjid, a mosque in the holy Hindu city of Ayodhya. (Courtesy of *India Tribune*.)

A unity march on Devon Avenue was organized in August 2001 by teen participants in the Indo-American Center community-building project in order to reduce tension between Indian and Pakistani immigrants in the neighborhood. Holding signs and flags aloft are, clockwise from bottom left, Veena Iyer, Vyjayanthi Vadrevu, Taha Mahmood, Faisal Hadi, Mohammed Ali, Shahbaz Jaweedan, and Baseeruddin Mohammed. (Courtesy of Indo American Center.)

Former Indian Prime Minister Morarji Desai (seated, center) attended a reception organized by the Gujarati community in Chicago on May 25, 1985. Asian Indian organizations frequently invite dignitaries from India to attend functions in the Chicago area. (Photo by Mukul Roy.)

Jose Anthony, President of the Indo-American Chamber of Commerce, presents a memento to Hon. H.D. Deve Gowda, former Prime Minister of India, during his visit to Chicago in 2000. (Courtesy of *India Tribune*.)

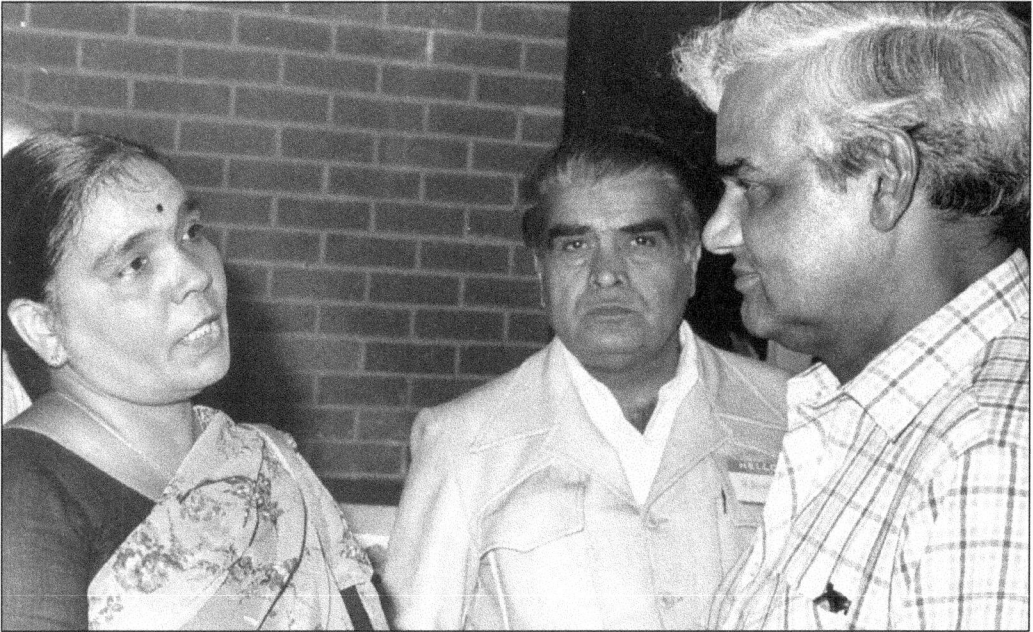

Atal Behari Vajpayee (right), a moderate leader of the Hindu nationalist Bharatiya Janata Party who became Prime Minister of India in 1996, conversed with Kiran Chaturvedi (left) and Dr. Raheja of the Hindi Literary Society when he visited Chicago during the late 1980s. (Photo by Mukul Roy.)

Sikandar Bakht, a senior Muslim official of the Bharatiya Janata Party who became India's Union Minister of Industry, addresses a gathering of Overseas Friends of the BJP at the Drake Hotel in Oak Brook in 1993. Other Indian political parties such as the Overseas Friends of Congress also seek to further their agenda by maintaining strong links with Indians abroad. (Courtesy of *India Tribune*.)

Gujarat Chief Minister Kesubhai Patel greets members of Chicago's Gujarati community during a visit organized by Niranjan Shah (seated, right). Visits by officials from Indian states have attracted investment in their regions by Indian Americans and led to developments such as the growth of the software industry in Bangalore and Hyderabad. (Courtesy of *India Tribune*.)

Darshan Singh Dhaliwal (seated, left) and other Sikh immigrants welcome Punjab Chief Minister Prakash Singh Badal (center) at a reception during his visit to Chicago. (Courtesy of Punjabi Cultural Society.)

The India National Conference held in Chicago in 1982 was attended by (left to right) Thomas Abraham, president of the national Federation of India Associations; Ranjit Ganguly; Basant Sathe, Indian cabinet minister for Information; Tirupatiah Tella, president of the Illinois chapter of the FIA; Arjun Singh, minister for Technology; and Indian Ambassador K.R. Narayanan, who became President of India in 1997. The conference was the first such gathering in the United States to be attended by a high-level government delegation from India. (Courtesy of Ranjit Ganguly.)

Chief Minister of Delhi Sheila Dixit and Chicago Mayor Richard M. Daley formalized the cultural and business links that had developed between the two cities by signing a Sister City agreement in October 2001. (Courtesy of *India Tribune*.)

123

Pushpika Freitas (left, facing group) meets with women of a cooperative in Mumbai who stitch clothing and other items offered through catalog sales of Northbrook-based MarketPlace: Handwork of India, which she founded as an outlet for their products. Many Non-Resident Indians (NRIs) actively support social and economic development efforts in India. (Courtesy of MarketPlace.)

Chicago Township rises from the rubble of Mewasa in Rapur *taluk* (district) following the devastation of the January 2001 earthquake in Gujarat. A fundraising effort spearheaded by Mafat Patel, Rohit Maniar, Dinesh Gandhi, and other business leaders led to the purchase of 22 acres of land where 160 duplex cottages, a medical clinic, school and community hall were constructed. The keys to the community were presented to the villagers in 2002. The Gujarat Relief Fund raised approximately $250,000 and was one of the most successful fund drives in Chicago's Indian community which typically responds generously to relief efforts in the homeland. (Courtesy of Mafat Patel.)

Select Readings
and Films about
Asian Indian Immigrants

Fresh voices in literature and film have appeared in the United States in conjunction with the growth of the Asian Indian community.

Bacon, Jean, **Life Lines: Community, Family, and Assimilation Among Asian Indian Immigrants**, New York: Oxford University Press, New York, 1996.
Through complex portraits of five immigrant families, Bacon shows how Asian Indians see themselves as a distinctive community within contemporary American society.

Kamdar, Mira, **Motiba's Tattoos: A Granddaughter's Journey Into Her Indian Family's Past**, New York: Public Affairs, Perseus Book Group, 2000.
Daughter of an American mother and Asian Indian father, Kamdar intriguingly describes life in India, which she first experienced as a child visiting her grandmother.

Khandelwal, Madhulika S. **Becoming American, Being Indian: An Immigrant Community in New York City** (The Anthropology of Contemporary Issues), Ithaca: Cornell University Press, 2002.
Khandelwal provides a profile of the largest Asian Indian community in the United States.

Maira, Sunaina Marr, **Desis in the House: Indian American Youth Culture in New York City** (Asian American History and Culture), Philadelphia: Temple University Press, 2002.
Maira amusingly exposes struggles of Asian Indian youth to be cool and authentic as they cope with racial, class, and gender identities.

Rangaswamy, Padma. **Namasté America: Indian Immigrants in an American Metropolis**, University Park: Penn State University Press, 2000 .
Interviews and documentation of the cultural, religious, linguistic, and socio-economic status of Asian Indian immigrants in Chicago provide revealing insights regarding their experiences.

Fiction

Desai, Boman, *The Memory of Elephants*, Chicago: The University of Chicago Press, 2000.
An Asian Indian immigrant to the U.S. acquaints readers with his heritage and Parsi customs as he depicts adventures of his ancestors and family members.

Divakaruni, Chitra Banerjee, *The Unknown Errors of Our Lives*, New York: Doubleday, 2001.
In her engaging short stories, Divakaruni illuminates the difficult adjustments of Asian Indian women as they adapt to life in the United States.

Lahiri, Jhumpa, *The Interpreter of Maladies*, New York: Houghton-Mifflin Mariner Books, 1999.
Jhumpa Lahiri's stories pull readers into the often bewildering core of immigrant experience.

Maira, Sunaina and Rajini Srikanth, Eds. *Contours of the Heart: South Asians Map North America*, Rutgers University Press, 1996.
This anthology explores interpretations of homeland and exile, of personal identity and familial duty in a lively way that reveals the complexities and ironies of living between cultures.

Rushdie, Salman & West, Elizabeth, Editors, *The Vintage Book of Indian Writing 1947–1997*, London: Vintage, 1997.
Excerpts from novels as well as short stories and essays by Asian Indian writers reflect the congeniality of the English language and the Indian sensibility.

Women of the South Asian Descent Collective, Editors, *Our Feet Walk the Sky, Women of the South Asian Diaspora*, San Francisco: Aunt Lute Books, 1993.
South Asian women immigrants and their daughters explore accommodation and alienation of ethnic heritage and tradition amidst the cultural diversity in the United States in this work.

Select Feature Films

Facets Multimedia, 1517 West Fullerton Avenue, Chicago 60614, 1-800-331-6197, www.facets.org is a convenient local source of DVD and videos.

ABCD, Krutin Patel
An Asian Indian mother yearns to have her "ABCD" (American Born Confused Desi—"one from our land"), young adult son and daughter maintain tradition in this poignant portrayal of the immigrant family.

Chutney Popcorn, Nisha Ganatra
When a young Asian Indian American woman decides to bear a child for her sister who is unable to conceive, her family becomes involved in an amusing family drama.

Karma Local, Darshan Bhagat
Bali, a young Indian immigrant working in his uncle's newsstand in New York is sucked into a vortex of misadventures when he agrees to hold a bag of loot for an eccentric regular customer.

Monsoon Wedding, Mira Nair
During an exuberant, lavish wedding celebration of a New Delhi bride and a Houston Asian Indian, a dramatic family situation tests family loyalty and solidarity.

About the
Indo-American Center

INDO-AMERICAN CENTER
6328 NORTH CALIFORNIA AVENUE
CHICAGO, IL 60659
773 973 4444
www.indoamerican.org

MISSION

The Indo-American Center's mission is to promote the well-being of Indo-Americans through services that facilitate their adjustment, integration and friendship with the wider society, nurture their sense of community, and foster appreciation for their culture and heritage.

The Indo-American Center was established in 1990 in response to the wide spectrum of needs in the South Asian immigrant community, the fastest growing Asian immigrant community in the Chicago area. While the Center's educational, social and charitable programs serve this very diverse population, its doors are open to everyone, regardless of ethnicity or religious or political affiliation.

IAC staff and volunteers work to smooth the transition process for immigrants as they adjust to life in their new homeland. In cooperation with the Immigration and Naturalization Service, the Center distributes visa forms and information. English and citizenship education classes are conducted in collaboration with the Illinois Literacy Foundation. Volunteer attorneys provide free legal services for the needy and college students and young professionals tutor, mentor and conduct social programs for youth. IAC also offers benefits counseling and activities for senior citizens.

The Center's outreach programs further interaction and understanding between the ethnic community and the wider society through special events, yoga classes and dance instruction. Collaboration with Chicago area public schools, the Field Museum of Natural History, the Chicago Historical Society, the Chicago Children's Museum, the Chicago Cultural Center and the City of Chicago Department of Tourism widens the reach of the Indo-American Center.

The Indo-American Center serves approximately 7000 persons each year. It is funded by donations from corporations, generous supporters in the community and grants from government agencies and private foundations including the Polk Brothers Foundation and the Chicago Community Trust.

Visit us at
arcadiapublishing.com

www.ingramcontent.com/pod-product-compliance
Lightning Source LLC
Chambersburg PA
CBHW080554110426
42813CB00006B/1304